Ghosts: True Tales of Eerie Encounters
Ghosts: More Eerie Encounters

"Belyk has his fingers on the preternatural pulse." —*Geist*

"An enjoyable and informative book." —*Times Colonist*

"Captivating (and chilling)." —*Vancouver Courier*

"As much as for believers, non-believers, and those who don't know what to believe, *Ghosts* is an interesting and mind-opening read that will trigger questions and discussions." —*The Concordian*

"The author has done a superb job of mining books and newspapers, as well as gathering accounts through interviews with participants." —*Canadian Book Review Annual*

Spirits of the West

OF THE

EERIE ENCOUNTERS FROM THE PRAIRIES TO THE PACIFIC

ROBERT C. BELYK

TouchWood
Editions

TouchWood Editions
touchwoodeditions.com

LIBRARY AND ARCHIVES CANADA CATALOGUING IN PUBLICATION
Belyk, Robert C., 1944–, author
Spirits of the west : eerie encounters from the Prairies
to the Pacific / Robert C. Belyk.

Issued in print and electronic formats.
ISBN 978-1-77151-039-4

1. Ghosts—Prairie Provinces. 2. Ghosts—British Columbia. 3. Haunted
places—Prairie Provinces. 4. Haunted places—British Columbia. I. Title.

BF1472.C3B445 2014   133.109712   C2013-906765-5

Editor: Marlyn Horsdal
Proofreader: Sarah Weber, Lightning Editorial
Design: Pete Kohut
Cover image: Courtesy of Diane Belyk
Author photo: Courtesy of Diane Belyk

Canadian Patrimoine
Heritage canadien

Canada Council Conseil des Arts
for the Arts du Canada

BRITISH COLUMBIA
ARTS COUNCIL

We gratefully acknowledge the financial support for our publishing activities
from the Government of Canada through the Canada Book Fund, Canada
Council for the Arts, and the province of British Columbia through the
British Columbia Arts Council and the Book Publishing Tax Credit.

MIX
Paper from
responsible sources
FSC
www.fsc.org   FSC® C016245

The interior pages of this book have been printed on 30% post-consumer
recycled paper, processed chlorine free, and printed with vegetable-based inks.

1 2 3 4 5 18 17 16 15 14

PRINTED IN CANADA

For Ewan and Shea

CONTENTS

PREFACE

If readers are looking for no more than ghost tales that will raise the hair on the back of their necks, make them sit up in bed, and hear every creak on the stairs, there are many good fictional books on the market that will meet their needs. Yet if readers want something more, something that has happened to living people during real hauntings, nothing is better than true ghost stories.

Almost all the chapters in this book have been compiled as a result of interviews with people who have experienced hauntings. In cases where the history of the events can be traced, knowing who the ghost is or why the incidents may be taking place adds another interesting dimension to the account. Often, no explanation for the ghost's strange behaviour is apparent, but this does not mean the reader will be disappointed, for in the realm of the supernatural a mystery unsolved is no less a great story.

Spirits of the West is the third book in a collection of ghost stories from western Canada. (The first book appeared in 1990 and is still available, in its second extended edition, as *Ghosts: True Tales of Eerie Encounters*. The second book was published in 1997 and is also available in an expanded version as *Ghosts: More Eerie Encounters*.)

1

One unfortunate difficulty with printed books is that they do not lend themselves to the inclusion of new material. There is a story in the first book about artist Hetty Fredrickson who, in the mid-1960s, lived in a house haunted by a very unpleasant ghost in the town of Chilliwack, British Columbia. At the time, the story of "Hetty's Ghost" was covered by the Vancouver press and was the subject of local radio talk shows. As a result of the publicity, people continually drove by Hetty's house, and crowds peered in the windows. She and her family finally had enough of the lack of privacy and moved to Vancouver Island, leaving the dwelling vacant for several months. After the house was eventually bought as a rental property, tenants reported unusual happenings. The haunted house was destroyed by fire in the mid-1970s.

I was surprised when, twenty years after Hetty's story first appeared in my book, Justin Wayne, who is the grandson of Pat Kammerer, contacted me. Mrs. Kammerer had lived in the house in 1957.

In 2010, I had an interesting interview with Mrs. Kammerer and her son Bill. More than fifty years after living there, he still has nightmares about being chased by a "thing." For Pat, one room was particularly frightening. Interestingly, by the time Hetty's story broke in the newspapers, Pat and her family had moved away and were unaware of the coverage it garnered. Coincidentally, also in 2010, I received more information, albeit second-hand, about another person who had stayed at the house later, to guard the property after Hetty left, and had several weird experiences there.

My point is simply that ghost stories are often never completely told. Although I researched the haunting of the Empress Theatre, in Fort Macleod, Alberta, exhaustively for *Spirits of the West*, I do not expect the ghostly incidents to stop. Active ghosts remain active.

I was fortunate to receive a considerable number of stories, many of which I have not had the time to include in this book. I have added more true ghost stories, as well as other material about *Spirits of the West* at Haunts West, www.hauntswest.com.

The screams of Colonel John Tayloe's daughter are still heard
as she falls from the second-floor balcony of Octagon House.
COURTESY OF THE LIBRARY OF CONGRESS, HABS DC, WASH, 8-36

ON GHOSTS AND HAUNTINGS

Ghosts are in the news not only at Halloween. One very public example of a ghost caught on film took place on December 14, 2012, when a New Orleans television news reporter on WGN-ABC, Vanessa Bolano, was before the cameras filming a feature on the Myrtles Plantation, 180 kilometres northwest of New Orleans. The Myrtles has long been called the most haunted house in the United States. After filming in the French Room, Vanessa and her crew were reviewing the tape and saw the image of a face appear near the bed and move up the wall. The apparition is likely to have been one of the thirteen ghosts said to haunt the old plantation house.

A little more than five years earlier, Seattle's famous Pike Place Market made the news with stories of its numerous ghosts. Karen McAleese, whose family owns Kells Irish Restaurant and Pub, was surprised when she saw a visitor wander out of the kitchen, which was for employees only. "He was a tall man who looked part black, with a suit jacket on," she told a reporter. Her surprise turned to shock when "he walked to the end of the bar and just kind of faded."[1] Elsewhere in the market, Nina Menon, proprietor of the Bead Zone, was in a heated telephone conversation when suddenly long strands of red beads tumbled from a wall hook and fell noisily to the floor. The curved metal rod that had held them remained in place and it was impossible for the bead strands to slide off the hook. These were only two of the happenings that occur almost routinely at the Pike Place Market.

The ghost experience is more common than is generally believed. In the United States, a 2009 CBS News poll revealed that twenty-two percent of Americans have encountered a ghost. Encounters with ghosts are now admitted and discussed openly, and it is the younger age group, people under forty-five, that more readily acknowledges such occurrences. An incredible twenty-nine percent of this age group admitted to encountering a ghost. The reason undoubtedly is that myriad reality television shows, watched primarily by younger people, appear to demonstrate that such entities do exist.

Paranormal phenomena also have a longer history than most people imagine. Ghost stories have been an integral part of Western cultural history for thousands of years. Plutarch, the Greek historian who wrote in the first and second centuries CE, recorded a legend that apparently had circulated for many years in Chaeronea, the small city where he was born. A criminal named Damon was murdered in the community baths. After his death, apparitions were seen there and ghostly sounds were heard so often that the citizens of Chaeronea were terrified. Eventually, the entrance to the bath was walled up, which seemingly ended the disturbances. Clearly, the notion of ghosts and haunted houses was well understood by the Greeks.

They believed that ghosts often returned to seek vengeance against their murderer or murderers. More than five centuries before Plutarch's account, one of the earliest ghost legends comes from the Battle of Marathon, during which ten thousand Athenians defeated a much larger Persian army that had arrived by ship on Greek soil. According to the Greek geographer Pausanias, writing long after the event, the Athenians claimed that a man wearing the garment of a peasant suddenly appeared in the midst of the battle. Wielding only a ploughshare, he fought with great strength and ferocity, killing many Persians. Then, as the battle ended, the warrior vanished. During its march from the sea to the Plains of Marathon, the Persian army would have laid waste to the land and killed many peasants who resisted the army's advance. In keeping with Greek beliefs, the Ghost of Marathon would have been a phantom seeking revenge against his Persian murderers.

Ghosts are not limited to Western culture. In China, belief in spirits has existed for thousands of years. Evil spirits are believed to come forth after dark and eschew the light. The existence of ghosts is also part of the culture of Japan, Thailand, and other nations of Southeast Asia; there are many supposedly haunted sites throughout the region. In the Hindu religion, ghosts are associated with people who have died violently or have not received the proper funeral rites.

What are ghosts? The obvious answer is that they are spirits of dead people who have returned to the world of the living. Like all issues concerning the paranormal, understanding ghosts is not that simple. In many cases the activities of the "ghost" are only a repetition of past events. The repeated sound of footsteps on a staircase, for example, may be an event that happens so often that researchers usually consider it to be only a minor haunting (although it may be very frightening to the people who live in the house).

When repeated sounds involve more than footsteps, however, it may be a different story. Washington DC's famous Octagon House is claimed to be haunted by the ghost of one of Colonel John Tayloe's daughters. It is said that during the British occupation of Washington in the War of 1812, the young woman fell in love with a British officer. By consorting with the enemy, she had betrayed her father. When rumours of the affair reached him, he waited one night for her on the balcony near the second-floor landing. When she returned after her tryst with her lover, she quietly made her way up the stairs toward her room, but her father stepped forward and confronted her. When she admitted that she loved the enemy soldier, a terrible argument ensued, ending only when the colonel pushed his daughter over the balcony rail.[2] Since then, residents and guests have heard her dreadful scream, followed by a sickening thud as her body strikes the floor below. This ghost is an example of a residual haunting, in which an event is replayed.

Often, though, paranormal activity is the result of conscious actions. On occasion, there appears to be a transcendental response to an occurrence in the natural world. A very unusual conscious haunting took place in 1942 in Nogales, Arizona, on the Mexican border. When immigration officer Gordon St. Thomas and his wife and children first moved into what had once been the quarters for officers in the former army outpost, they felt they were not alone. What was particularly interesting about the unseen resident was that he was fastidious. When St. Thomas returned from work and carelessly tossed his cap on a chair, he would later find it hanging on the hat rack. Items left around the home would be returned to their proper places. The ghost appeared to be against smoking—packets with cigarettes still in them constantly turned up in the wastepaper basket.

The ghost was also helpful. After a late shift, St. Thomas returned from work and, not wanting to wake his wife, decided to sleep in the spare room. He had climbed into bed but had not fallen asleep when he felt something tugging on his foot. He arose and turned on the light to discover he was alone. However, on the ceiling over the bed was a scorpion. Nocturnal creatures, scorpions seek dark places in the day, and had the creature dropped onto the bed, as was likely, St. Thomas could have sustained a nasty or even fatal sting. He was thankful for the intervention of the resident ghost.

On rare occasions, these conscious entities attempt to contact family or friends directly. They usually want to pass on a message, such as where they had hidden valuables. In some cases the ghost appears seeking justice. Probably the most famous case occurred in Portland, Oregon, after the supposed suicide of Lieutenant James Sutton in 1907. At the time of his death, James was a cadet at the United States Naval Academy in Annapolis, Maryland. At the moment his mother received word of her son's passing, she saw him standing before her. "Momma," he said, "I never killed myself."[3] The murderers were other cadets who made James's death look like suicide, he told her. For several months Mrs. Sutton continued to be visited by her son, who described his death in detail, providing facts that Mrs. Sutton would otherwise not have known. Two years later, she had her son's body exhumed, and the wounds the young man had received, which were not mentioned in the original report, were discovered. Although he apparently named his murderers, no charges were ever laid, and justice was never done.

It would appear that ghosts are evidence of the existence of life after death. Yet the question remains, what kind of existence? In many cases, even when the identity of the ghost seems certain, its intellect often appears limited. Frequently, the ghost of a man or woman, who in life was serious and thoughtful, resorts to childish behaviours. Ghosts appear to enjoy playing ridiculous pranks. Although not poltergeists, such ghosts have some of their characteristics.

Crisis apparitions are another ghost category. These entities appear or otherwise make their presence known at or near the time of death. Many stories are passed down through a family and concern an ancestor who died at a distant location and whose apparition is briefly seen by a close family member. These are ghosts with a message.[4]

The perception of a ghostly presence can include from one to four of the five senses. (I have never found a case of a person tasting a ghost, but anything is possible.) The order in which they most often occur is described below.

Auditory: By far the most frequent psychical events are sounds, including everything from unexplained loud noises to phantom footsteps on stairs. Often auditory events are the first indication of a haunting that will involve the other senses.

Visual: The sighting of a ghost in any form, including orbs (small spheres of light), ill-defined shapes, semi-transparent human figures, and full-bodied apparitions, is not as common as most people believe. It may require considerable energy for a phantom to materialize, which is perhaps beyond the ability of most ghostly entities.

Olfactory: Smells from pleasant to foul sometimes accompany other sensory perceptions of ghosts. Unlike natural occurrences, when odours diffuse gradually within the environment, these smells are often very clearly defined. One step beyond the affected area may mean the sudden cessation of the smell.

Tactile: This sense includes a broad range of perceptions, from feeling a hand resting on one's arm to walking into what appears to be an unseen body. "Cold shafts," or unexplained rapid drops in temperature within a distinctly defined area, are also commonly associated with the tactile sense.

There are, of course, many other indications that a place is haunted. Ghosts, for example, seem to have little difficulty manipulating electrical and electronic circuitry. Lights may turn on and off without human intervention, channels on the television may change, or the telephone may ring for no apparent reason.

HAUNTINGS

A haunting is the active manifestation of a paranormal presence. In many people's minds, the haunted house is where ghosts are found. Hundreds of movies have featured a typical old house where malevolent spirits dwell, waiting for some unsuspecting person or family to move in. That, of course, is Hollywood. Most entities are beings that, although often frightening, do not injure people.

Hauntings are not limited to houses—pubs often have the kind of spirits not limited to the shelves behind the bar. Hotels and bed and breakfasts sometimes have ghosts. Indeed, it is surprising that these places do not have more resident ghosts. Within the rooms of such places, people live and occasionally die under very emotional circumstances. Until recently, owners and managers have often attempted to deny that paranormal activities have occurred in their hostelries. However, ghostly behaviour is hard to cover up, and many operators now admit that their building has non-paying guests.

Museums, stores, offices, and even police stations are also the locus of ghost activity. Ghosts frequently inhabit the wards of hospitals, whether general or psychiatric. Wycombe General Hospital, in Buckinghamshire, England, was the scene of a haunting in which the call bell would ring even when no patients were in the room.

In Elizabeth, New Jersey, the Elizabeth General Medical Center's Newborn Nursery is supposed to be haunted by the ghost of a woman in white. The Peoria State Hospital, in Bartonville, Illinois, which closed in 1973, is said to still have the ghosts of patients who lived and died at this former psychiatric hospital.

Ghosts are not found in graveyards as often as many people believe. Novice ghosts hunters, particularly, spend long and fruitless nights in such locations, anticipating meeting a departed soul. However, there are a number of well-known cemetery ghosts. Resurrection Cemetery in the Chicago suburb of Justice, Illinois, is believed to be the burial place of Resurrection Mary, the city's most famous ghost. Although there is probably some truth behind the stories that date to the 1940s, it is now difficult to separate the facts from the legend of this beautiful blond girl in the white dress who tries to hitch a ride to the O. Henry Ballroom. Indeed, even today, motorists claim to see Mary in the vicinity of Resurrection Cemetery. Archer Woods Cemetery in Chicago is the site of the Sobbing Woman, who is occasionally seen near the entrance. Why she is crying is a matter of conjecture.

Actress Virginia Rappe, who seemingly was no stranger to the casting couch, is claimed to haunt Hollywood's Forever Cemetery. Her death, supposedly under the body of the famous silent film comedian Roscoe "Fatty" Arbuckle in 1921, created a sensation in Hollywood. After three trials for manslaughter, the rotund actor was finally acquitted, but his career was in ruins. Many historians today believe that Arbuckle was the innocent target of an extortion scheme that went wrong. At Rappe's gravesite in Forever Cemetery, witnesses claim to have heard a woman sobbing—sounds that appear to come from *under* the plot. Visitors have also felt a shaft of cold air near her burial site.

VOYAGEURS

Voyageurs are travelling ghosts that have haunted one location and have been able to "hitch a ride" when people move. Usually one of those people is particularly sensitive to what sociologists would describe as the super-empirical reality: there is a connection, albeit reluctant, between that person and the entity. These ghosts often do not stay long at their new address—they move back to their original haunt or simply fade away.

POLTERGEISTS

Poltergeists do not fit neatly into the category of ghosts, but a brief mention of the subject is necessary. Poltergeist is a German word that means "noisy ghost." Objects typically move around the room without physical intervention, and raps and occasionally loud noises are heard. Parapsychologists have theorized that such activity is the result of a unexplained force called psychokinesis, or PK. One significant difference between a poltergeist and a ghost is that in the former case, there is never any perception that one is facing an eerie presence—the hair on a person's arm, for example, does not stand on end. Another is that the poltergeist event often arises spontaneously, continues for a limited time, and then abates or stops abruptly. Until fairly recently, parapsychologists believed that it was necessary for one person to be the focus of poltergeist activity, but recent research has revealed that this might not be the case.

SCIENCE AND THE PARANORMAL

The research of a Canadian scientist, Dr. Michael Persinger, is interesting in that it leads toward a new direction in understanding the biological basis of psychic experiences. The cognitive neuroscientist postulated that exposure to even low ranges of electromagnetic fields and ultra low frequency sound will produce hallucinations of a religious or supernatural nature in some individuals. Recently his work has led toward the hypothesis that seven-hertz magnetic fields increase telepathic abilities in test subjects. Although the seven-hertz field increases responses, telepathy has always been a means of communication within the human species—that is, given the right conditions. He prefaced one lecture by citing a case study in which a family member had been aware that something was terribly wrong at the instant of the unexpected death of a loved one many kilometres away. Not surprisingly, Persinger's work remains controversial.[5]

Even more revolutionary, and far beyond the pale of orthodox science, is the theory that ghosts are in essence a form of electromagnetic energy. Empirical evidence suggests that there is a relationship between very active hauntings and high-energy fields. Some researchers believe ghosts require a lot of energy to manifest their presence.

Today, greater interest in the paranormal has led to a dramatic increase in groups dedicated to finding ghosts wherever they may be. Although it is not a new theory, explorers of the unknown accept that ghosts exist as energy and that it is measurable. Spurred on by television shows like *Ghost Hunters* and *Ghost Adventures*, these amateur groups are turning to technology to "prove" the existence of discarnate entities. Electromagnetic field "ghost detectors" are readily available at a low price on the Internet.

While parapsychologists consider these ghost-hunting groups unscientific in their approach, it should be noted that they have directed their attention to an area that would otherwise not have been investigated. Parapsychology is the orphan child of academia; few parapsychology courses are offered at North American universities, and almost no funds are available for research in this field. The information that amateur organizations gather is worthwhile; many of the larger, well-organized groups are reputable and certainly contribute to the empirical evidence that ghosts exist.

It should also be mentioned that today, the Internet contains many fraudulent photos. Until the age of digital photography, it was difficult, though not impossible, to fake ghost photos. A person would have to be skilled in the use of the darkroom to produce a double negative. With the advent of Photoshop and similar programs, the trickery is simple. (It is therefore incumbent on reputable researchers to trust the source of their photos and be assured of their validity before publication.)

Since 1882, when a group of British scientists and academics first attempted to apply the tools of science to the study of ghosts, progress has, at the least, been slow. This may not be surprising, given that these entities have not lent themselves to investigations under controlled laboratory conditions. However, science may at last be making the first tentative steps toward investigating the processes underlying the psychic realm. Probably of greatest importance is a change in public opinion. With the subject now openly discussed, more will be learned about the nature of these singularly mysterious phenomena. It is possible to conclude that unless one makes the ridiculous assumption that a significant percentage of the population is subject to hallucinations, humans do sometimes find themselves face to face with these strange beings called ghosts.

The Empress Theatre is often listed among the
most haunted theatres in North America.
COURTESY OF DIANE BELYK

CHAPTER ONE

HAUNTED ATTRACTIONS

NOW APPEARING AT THE EMPRESS

The Empress Theatre in Fort Macleod, Alberta, can claim several distinctions that set it apart from other similar venues. Its excellent acoustics have attracted many of Canada's top musicians, who usually would not play a theatre with such a limited seating capacity. Also, it is this country's oldest continuously operating theatre, as its beautiful art deco decor suggests. Yet chillingly, of particular interest to readers of this book, the Empress also holds the distinction of being Canada's most haunted theatre.

During the first year of the twentieth century, the community leaders of Fort Macleod (then Macleod), 165 kilometres south of Calgary, saw their town as the centre of a great railway boom that would exploit the wealth of mineral-rich southwestern Alberta. The coming of the First World War, though, brought an end to the inflow of capital, and rail lines that had existed only on paper were never begun. The town that had been built on dreams drifted on in the dust of failed promotions.

In 1910, when confidence in the future of Fort Macleod was at its height, entrepreneur T.B. Martin began construction of the Empress Theatre, in the same block as the elegant Queen's Hotel. The 450-seat brick-and-sandstone structure was built with an eye to the future, when the population of the community would be far greater. Completed in 1912 as an opera house, it soon became part of the Famous Players theatre franchise, which presented live concerts and vaudeville acts that toured North America. Eventually, silent films became part of the entertainment and, by the early 1930s, movies with sound were the main feature.

The Empress Theatre passed through many owners until 1937, when a businessman, Dan Boyle, purchased it. Boyle's timing could not have been better, because the Great Depression, which had devastated the Prairie provinces, was coming to an end. During his ownership, he modernized the theatre and added a one-hundred-seat balcony. Boyle's sudden death in 1963 brought an end to the theatre's most successful period. Competition from television was strong, and theatre seats remained unfilled. Moreover, the three-block downtown core was badly in need of revitalization.

In 1982, the residents of the community organized to restore the downtown core, as well as to recreate the Royal Canadian Mounted Police outpost that gave the town its name. One of the first buildings to be renovated and partially restored was the venerable Empress Theatre.

Major structural changes were made to enlarge the basement area, which now contains the green room (the actors' lounge) and new dressing rooms. Among the many enhancements were new curtains, carpets, and seats. In 1987, the theatre was taken over by the Provincial Historic Area Society. Work continued on the building through the late 1980s.

As early as the 1960s, rumours had been circulating around Fort Macleod that the Empress Theatre was haunted. At the time, management did its best to discourage such tales, fearing that stories of ghosts would keep customers away. The renovations in the late 1980s dramatically increased the scale of paranormal activities. Before the dust had settled on the changes to the Empress, it was clear that the work had brought back ghosts from the past.

One of the early indications that something unusual was happening began when work on the theatre had hardly started. To keep out intruders, a security company installed motion detectors at different locations throughout the theatre. Although it is common for false alarms to be triggered during the set-up of the system, it seemed impossible to get the "bugs" out of the intruder alarm. During the late night and early morning hours, calls from company monitors frequently brought police and theatre management to the Empress. On investigation, no intruder was ever found, and the unexplained triggering of the alarms has become one of the hallmarks of the Empress Theatre haunting.

In the mid-1980s, an event had many theatre people scratching their heads. A member of the Great West Theatre Company, Jay Russell, was alone in the theatre and decided to explore the interesting old building. He began by walking along the hallway that led from the lobby down the rickety stairs to the area where the old dressing rooms were located near the boiler room.

Before renovations were completed, the theatre had had no proper green room; actors were forced to wait in the boiler room while offstage. Beside the boiler room was a space with a steel door that was dubbed the "swamp cooler room," probably because water seepage produced an unpleasant smell. (This difficulty was overcome when the theatre was raised and a new foundation poured.) Because the theatre was short of space, the dry portion of the room had been used for storage.

The door to the storage area was latched and could be opened only from the boiler room. The swamp cooler room was not wired for electricity, so the only light came indirectly from the boiler room. In the shadows, Russell could see an old organ that had been disassembled. Wanting a closer look at the instrument, he propped the door wide open so he could go inside. He entered the room and began walking toward the organ. He recalled his experience:

> I reached into the dark, and it's getting darker and darker, and I have my hand extended out trying to reach this old keyboard or whatever it is. And just as I touch it, there's this big laugh behind me. Like someone is pulling the funniest joke in the world on me. It wasn't spooky; it was just this big belly laugh. And all of a sudden, the prop on my door was gone and the door slams shut. And then thump, thump, thump, thump up the stairs. Someone was laughing and running up the stairs.[1]

Russell remained locked in the dark room for more than an hour. During the first few minutes, he thought someone in the theatre company was playing a joke on him, but no one would have left him in that unpleasant place so long. Moreover, the stairs were extremely noisy, and while he had heard someone run away up the steps, he had heard no sound of anyone coming down. It clearly made no sense.

When Jim Layton began cleanup work at the theatre following the renovations, he did not believe in ghosts. His experiences at the Empress, however, led him to reassess his opinion. In 1989, management hired him to wax the scuffed floors and vacuum the dust-laden carpets. The tasks had to be done after the patrons had left for the evening, which meant he was usually alone in the theatre.

One night, when he was sitting in the basement green room

waiting for the floors to dry, his concentration on the magazine that he was reading was abruptly broken when he heard noises coming from somewhere upstairs near the front of the building. Believing that someone may have been trying to break in, he checked the lobby, but there was no sign of an intruder. Unsettled, he returned to his chores.

The next night, instead of sitting in the green room while the floors dried, he took a seat in the lobby. This time a clatter erupted from the basement, from the same general area as the green room. "I don't get scared very easily," Layton remembered, "but I was out of there really quick."[2]

Diana Segboer was involved in administration of the Empress from 1988 until 1997. Her first inkling that there was something unusual began when she visited the theatre to fill out the order for items needed for the concession booth. As she entered from the street through the big glass doors, she called out, "I'm here," in the event that the janitor was still in the building. Receiving no answer, she entered the concession booth and pulled down the glass window that secured the small area. As she was completing the concession orders, she heard footsteps coming from the corridor that led from the basement to the lobby. Diana was not concerned, for she assumed it was Mike, the janitor, coming up the stairs to say hello. As she worked, the footsteps drew closer until they entered the lobby. When the footsteps stopped in front of the concession booth, Diana looked up, expecting to see Mike's familiar face. She was shocked to discover that no one was standing by the open window. She recalled, "I finished my order and I just booted it right out of there."[3]

Juran Greene, who was the first manager after the restoration of the Empress, soon found that when he made evening visits to the theatre, he was not alone. One of the strangest things occurred one night when he was walking across the stage. Two ladders that were positioned against the wall at the back of the stage suddenly toppled forward. Without someone physically changing their centres of gravity, there could be no logical explanation for the incident. To his credit, Juran maintained his composure and told his unseen visitor that he was going to be around the theatre and that it would have to accept this fact.

There were other unnerving events. He was working late one night in his downstairs office, engrossed in his task, when he became aware of footsteps on the old floorboards above him. New on the job, and thinking someone may have had a legitimate reason to be in the building at that late hour, Juran called out, asking who it was. His question was met by silence. Concerned now, he walked upstairs to where the sounds originated. The room was in darkness, and when he switched on the light, no one was there.

Even more upsetting to Juran was what he discovered in the room. New carpets had recently been laid over the old floorboards, and on the pile was a thick layer of dust. If someone had walked across the floor, it would have been impossible not to leave footprints. But amazingly the dust remained undisturbed.

After sundown when he was frequently alone, Juran continued to experience the sound of footsteps in the building. There were of course skeptics who offered superficial explanations. One such "reason" for the sounds particularly rankled Juran. He said, "They used to say the building was settling. But then how does a building settle when it sounds like someone is walking on the floor?"[4]

Juran was not the only new member of staff to know that something peculiar was happening at the Empress. Assistant manager Terry Veluw first witnessed what for more than twenty years would be one of the commonest occurrences of the haunting. All over the building, lights in different areas would turn on or off at odd times, seemingly on their own. It was impossible to blame ancient electrical circuits—new wiring had been installed during renovations. Moreover, this occurred not in one or two isolated circuits, but throughout the newly wired theatre. These episodes happen so frequently that they are now almost taken for granted.

Terry also witnessed odd events relating to the intercom system, which emitted eerie sounds. "It was like somebody talking," she said, "but it wasn't in an understandable language. But it was somebody making noises."[5] The sounds were not restricted to the intercom.

As mentioned earlier, false alarms have been a continuing problem in the theatre. Although the electronic alarm system has been upgraded over the years, it is still frequently set off at times in the absence of human intruders. During the years when she was the chairperson of the Empress, Diana Segboer was usually the first person the security company contacted when the system was activated. What was particularly annoying, she recalls, was that "it would go off at odd times at night."[6] Once, in the early hours of the morning, she received a call saying that a sensor had been triggered. Because it was board policy that two of its members respond to a call, Diana phoned a fellow director, Joyce Bonertz, to ask her to accompany her.

As she drove to the theatre, a melody was going through Joyce's head. "It was a World War II song," she said, "but I can't remember now what it was called."[7]

The two board members met at the theatre, where they unlocked the main door and then passed through the lobby. "Joyce was always a hummer," Diana recalled.[8] When they reached the stage, she was humming a tune. She continued humming until they completed their investigation and returned to the lobby.

Joyce remembers that "a person or entity was whistling the same song." It had picked up the last bars of the melody. Believing they had found the intruder, she turned to Diana and said, "There's somebody in the theatre." But there was no one else anywhere in the building. "I didn't feel frightened at the time," Joyce said, "but afterwards I kind of fell apart."[9]

In the early years, the green room, which also serves as the boardroom, was a hot spot of activity. Diana and several others witnessed two coffee cups rise several centimetres off the table. Then, to everyone's amazement, they glided the length of the table before settling down again on the wood surface. For Diana, it was simply another event to add to the growing list of paranormal experiences at the Empress.

At one point, the theatre's governing board faced a serious personnel crisis that divided the community. Diana recalled that, during one meeting at the theatre, a heated argument broke out. "All of a sudden people stopped talking. We heard someone crying." The sound seemed to come from the green room, but it was impossible to determine where it originated.

Sometime later, a similar incident occurred when members of the theatre company heard whimpering sounds coming from one of the dressing rooms. They knocked on the door, but there was no response. Concerned, they tried to turn the doorknob, but the room was locked. Finally they were forced to break in, but to their surprise, not a living soul was in the dressing room.

Larger dressing rooms with showers had been added on the opposite side of the corridor from the existing tiny cubicles. The new rooms were certainly an improvement, but people taking showers were often aware of a cold wind that seemed to rise out of nowhere. It was more than a breeze—it blew with great force through the shower stalls. Then just as quickly, it would stop. It was unnatural, for there were no vents within the stalls. It was as if someone had opened the shower door and then, after a short time, closed it again in an invasion of privacy. Today, the cold shower wind seems to have died away.

A continuing occurrence is the pattering of tiny feet along one of the aisles in the auditorium. Unlike the heavy tread that is often heard in the corridor and on the stairs leading to the basement, these are the sounds made by a small child running up and down in the theatre.

Who are the ghosts that haunt the Empress? The most likely candidate is Ed, a janitor who worked there during the 1930s. Ed had a second job at the Macleod Auction House, where he shovelled out the cattle pens. The odour of manure mixed with the smell of cigar smoke in the theatre suggests Ed may be the ghost.[10] Ed is believed to have been a burly man who often wore a cowboy hat. Adding to the lore, it is claimed he died behind the auction house under mysterious circumstances.

A strange story that apparently happened more than twenty years ago concerns two young women who were late for a performance they very much wanted to see. They were gratified to find that someone was still sitting in the ticket booth when they arrived, an older man wearing a cowboy hat. Even though it was past the time for sales, the man sold them two tickets to the live show. After the event, the women wanted to thank him. They found the woman who usually sold tickets in the lobby, and asked her about her ticket booth replacement. No one had taken her place she said, and she certainly did not sell the two women tickets. When they produced the correct stubs, the volunteer was mystified. She had no memory of taking money from these patrons, yet the ticket sales matched the cash total exactly.

One of Ed's occasional haunts has been the women's

restroom. Not long after the theatre was renovated, a witness described seeing a heavy-set man with hairy arms. Interestingly, Abraham Segboer, an older resident of Fort Macleod, once recalled his childhood visits to the Empress Theatre, where the janitor had very hairy arms.

Another sighting of the restroom ghost happened in 1993, when Lisa Regan, then twelve years old, was rehearsing at the Empress for her dance school's yearly recital. Her godmother sent her to the women's restroom to straighten her hair, a few unruly strands of which had come undone. The restroom stalls were directly behind the sinks and mirrors, and Lisa was so preoccupied with her task that she did not notice the open cubicles behind her. Suddenly she was aware of a man reflected in the mirror. "He was sitting on the toilet and just watching me."[11] She described him as in his late thirties or early forties with brown hair, wearing a dark brown sweater and blue jeans. He was a solid, full-bodied apparition that looked so real Lisa believed he was a living person. This idea was quickly dispelled when she turned to face her watcher. The stall was empty.

Frightened, the young dancer ran down the stairs to the dressing rooms, where she told her dance group about her encounter with the ghost. Lisa's account was soon referred to the theatre's staff member who consulted a logbook. "The woman," Lisa said, "came down later and told me that somebody earlier had described him in the same way I did."

Although the blue jeans would have been in keeping with the dress of Ed the janitor, Lisa did not recall a cowboy hat, nor did she mention that he was a burly individual. The sweater he was wearing would have concealed his hairy arms. The stall door, though, would have partially obscured a full view of the entity. Lisa never had the impression that the ghost was angry, simply curious.

After death, at least, Ed may have become a fan of live theatre. During rehearsals, there have been reports of actors witnessing an older, burly man wearing a cowboy hat sitting in seat FF1 in the balcony.

In 2006, during a matinee performance of a play, the show lacked the energy that typified other performances; the actors had been celebrating late the previous evening. Cast member Andy Jenkins remembered that "in the middle of a show we had an actor miss an entrance. Then suddenly the curtains closed and all the lights went out."[12]

While one might have thought that the technician had accidentally closed the show, Andy said, "What was really weird was that from a sitting position up in the [technician's] booth, you can't do the lights and the curtains simultaneously. It was not as though somebody could bump something to make these things happen." Furthermore, the following year, when an actor forgot his lines in the middle of a monologue, the lights suddenly went out, plunging the stage into darkness. "It is very rare to have two bad shows like those," Andy observed.

One of the most frightening events was a phone call from the dead. The Empress's former development director, Terry Daniel, often worked during odd hours at his desk in the ticket office, which is two doors down the street from the theatre. The same four telephone lines connect both buildings, and incoming or outgoing calls on one telephone line would light up a telephone's active buttons in both locations. Often Terry arrived early in the morning to find one of the theatre's phone lines lit up, even when no one was in the theatre and the alarm system was still activated. At first he thought it was likely that a previous call had not been disconnected properly. Then someone would phone him on a line that was apparently in use—a seemingly impossible situation. These episodes only foreshadowed a bizarre occurrence that left Terry truly discomfited. He recalled the event, which occurred one evening when he was working late:

> I was in the office by myself and the phone rang and when I answered it this voice sounded like it was coming from nowhere. It was really weird, really raspy. It said, "How do I get out of here?" I said, "Where are you?" I thought it was someone in the theatre trying to phone out. "You have to punch one of the outside lines," I said. "In the theatre you just push the button for line one, two, three . . ." Then the connection kind of dwindled on me. It just seemed to disappear.[13]

Terry replaced the receiver. The call left him nonplussed. Before he had time to think about it, the phone rang again and he answered it. The voice on the other end of the line said again, "How do I get out of here?"

"Where are you?" Terry repeated.

"At the back of the theatre," the raspy voice said.

Assuming that someone had been locked in, Terry quickly walked the two doors down the street to the Empress. On the stage was a group of teenagers, participants in a short introductory theatre program under the direction of Jeremy Mason.

Terry's first thought was that one of the young people had gone to the back of the theatre, where the phones were, to play a prank. But the area was in total darkness, and had one of the actors sneaked away, Jeremy would have been aware of his missing student and of the lights being turned on at the rear of the theatre. Also, Terry's quick arrival meant that it was unlikely that anyone would have had time to turn off the lights and find his way through the dark back to the stage. What makes the idea of a prank even more unlikely is that it would have been necessary to dial the internal three-digit number of the office—a number that the students would not have readily known.

One may wonder if Ed the critic was having difficulty enduring the energetic yet inexperienced young actors in rehearsal and was looking for a means of escaping his long-standing haunt. Hence his call: "How do I get out of here?"

In his new capacity as tour director, Andy Jenkins shows visitors the beautifully restored building and relates many of the interesting stories associated with it. One such account concerns disembodied tap dancers that had been heard performing late-night numbers on the stage. Visitors have snapped photos and frequently caught images of orbs. These photos did not usually impress their tour guide. The low-light conditions inside the theatre combined with the built-in flashes on digital cameras could produce such "floating" artifacts. One photo, however, surprised him. Evenly spaced across the stage were twelve semicircular objects that looked like the tutus worn by ballet dancers. The picture left Andy unsettled. No ballet troupe had ever performed at the Empress, but over the years, many of the local dance schools have used the theatre for their yearly recitals.

Some of these events, like the sound of a child running down the aisle of the theatre and the click, click, click of tap dancers on stage, are residual hauntings. As has been mentioned, such incidents are like a video or tape recorder playing back an earlier event. Thus, there is no intelligence to such events—witnesses simply see the same images or hear the same sounds repeatedly. Most occurrences at the Empress, though, are the result of intelligent beings.

This is not a ghost captured in this photo of the Empress
Theatre's back stairs, but an artifact created by reflected light.
COURTESY OF DIANE BELYK

In some sightings, the distance from the source and the reduced lighting in the auditorium have made it impossible to provide much of a physical description of the entity haunting the theatre. When Andy Jenkins began working in the summer performance program at the Empress, he did not believe in ghosts. However, over the years, he witnessed so many eerie happenings that he has changed his mind. In the early hours of the morning, in the summer of 2007, he and his friend Adam Cope were painting a set on stage when they heard someone walking. Andy recalled:

> I heard somebody go up the stairs toward the balcony. And then I saw a person walk under the exit sign. The light wasn't on in the [balcony] hallway, but there was light bleed from the projection booth. I couldn't make out who it was but I saw somebody walk by there. I immediately thought it was Chris, our technician, stopping by to fix something. I called up, "Hey Chris, it's two in the morning. What are you doing? We'll fix it later." There was no response, and then I saw a figure in the projection booth walk from window to window. I looked over at my friend Adam who said he heard and saw the same thing.[14]

Believing that it was a homeless person who had found an entry into the theatre, the two men went quickly to the projection booth to investigate. But no one was there.

The current janitor has apparently seen another entity in the Empress. Although she declined to be interviewed, several reliable sources have reported she saw the ghost of a woman near the dressing rooms and the green room. The phantom wore a formal dress flared from the waist. It has been speculated that the person may have been the pianist who played accompaniment to the silent films, or even Edna, the wife of Dan Boyle. It is possible that this woman was the source of the cries and sobs heard in the basement.

Some people have speculated that Boyle himself could be responsible for many of the happenings attributed to Ed the janitor. For more than twenty years, Boyle was president of the Fort Macleod Rodeo Association, and it seems likely that he would have worn a cowboy hat at times. He also had a penchant for cigars. Rather than resembling the heavy-set man often described as haunting the theatre, Boyle was a tall, thin individual who was a dapper dresser.

Whether it is Ed or another entity, the Prankster is one of the most active ghosts haunting the Empress. This presence seems to have an unusual sense of humour. Following movie nights, volunteers are charged with cleanup duty, which involves picking up the candy wrappers, soft drink cups, and popcorn containers. In the process the seats will be pushed into their upright positions to allow vacuuming of the rows. Often, to their surprise, the workers will find the seats pushed down again as if they were occupied. This is not easily explained, for they remain firmly in the up position, and moving them down again requires some force. This moving of the seats was noted as early as 1989 and continues to this day.

Another of the ghost's favourite tricks is to wait until volunteers have picked up the trash from the auditorium and emptied it into containers in the basement. When they arrive the next day, all of the trash will be strewn over the floor. Not surprisingly, the volunteers do not appreciate the Prankster's sense of humour.

While the ghostly activity at the Empress has never been

malevolent, the Prankster seems to enjoy playing tricks on people connected with the theatre. Yet the haunting of the Empress has involved more than practical jokes. In one case, the dead came to the assistance of the living. During a visit to the theatre, one of the society board members stepped backwards off the stage. Although the distance to the floor is only a little more than a metre, the board member was no longer young, and she could have been badly injured. The woman did not srike the floor though; something broke her fall. She said it felt as if she had fallen onto a soft body.

In the early hours of the morning of November 19, 2011, an inexplicable event left theatre people very puzzled. The building's intruder alarm system was triggered again. A video camera that was set to capture any attempted entry at the fire door did not pick up movement in that area, but it did record something strange. The wide-angle lens caught a white wispy form moving across the stage. It is visible for only the briefest time, but its appearance adds to the great volume of evidence that the Empress is one of North America's most haunted theatres.

Theatres are often closely connected with ghosts. Many researchers have suggested that the energy generated by actors during live performances might precipitate these events. Further, the emotional responses of the audience that seep over the years into older theatres like the Empress may have some association with ghostly manifestations.

THE GHOSTS OF HELL'S GATE

Not far from the little community of Boston Bar, British Columbia, two hundred kilometres northwest of Vancouver on the Trans-Canada Highway, is one of the province's most spectacular natural attractions, where the water of the mighty Fraser River roils in great white plumes as it pounds against the rocks. At this, the river's narrowest point, the walls slope inward, trapping the flow within a mere thirty-five-metre gap. From the time of the earliest European exploration, this place of nature's fury was called the "Gate of Hell." Indeed, it is also a place with a violent history, where people of many races have met untimely deaths.

Before the completion of the Hell's Gate Airtram in 1971, the ghosts of this isolated chasm were usually left alone. Now, though, the gondola ride above the Fraser River and the site itself provide visitors with not only a breathtaking aerial view of this natural wonder, but also, on occasion, a glimpse into the world of the supernatural.

Simon Fraser, the first European to make the descent of the river that bears his name, discovered the perils of Hell's Gate. Setting out from Fort George on May 28, 1808, with his party of twenty-three explorers in four canoes, he had little idea of the danger ahead. When he reached the sheer walls and thundering waters of the lower Fraser Canyon, he realized that this was where his anticipated voyage to the Pacific might end. Hell's Gate made the portages (the hauling of canoes over land) extremely difficult.

The Cariboo gold rush in 1862 brought many miners to the goldfields near Barkerville, and the wagon road constructed by the Royal Engineers and private contractors followed the canyon. Although the death toll among the workers near Hell's Gate is unknown, the blasting of the narrow road out of the sheer canyon walls probably cost many lives. Further deaths occurred after 1879 with the building of the Canadian Pacific Railway (CPR) through the canyon.

The Hell's Gate Airtram that spans the gorge is in two sections. On the east side, or upper level, are some offices, the control area, the ticket booth, the boarding area, a small gift shop, and parking lots. The main attractions are on the lower, or terminal, level, which includes shops, a gold-panning site, and a fisheries exhibit. Most of the eerie activity takes place here on the west side of the Fraser.

Brian McKinney's father was an original shareholder in the airtram company, and now he and his sister Debbie manage the operation. Since the time Brian was ten years old, he has spent much of his life at the site, and he is very familiar with its history. Throughout their lives, Brian and Debbie have had no particular interest in the paranormal. "However," Brian recalled, "we often wondered about this area because at times it just kind of gave us the creeps. Not only at night, but during the day even."[15] When weird happenings took place, they simply attempted to come up with rational explanations. "We just had to blame it on something," Brian said.

All that changed one afternoon in late November of 2004. Although the attractions are open only between Easter and the Thanksgiving weekend, some clerical and maintenance personnel are on hand during the off-season. Brian was in his office in the upper level when a phone call came from the closed Simon Fraser's Café. On the other end of the line was Peter, one of the maintenance staff who had been working in the lower terminal.

"Hi, Brian. I'm just calling to find out is there anyone down here on the other side with me?"

"No," Brian said. "We're the only two here. Why do you ask?"

"Well, I was warming up my meal in the cafeteria and somebody walked behind me."

Puzzled, Brian said, "Are you sure?"

"I'm sure," Peter said. "I felt someone brush up against me. In fact I was so sure I actually did say, 'Sorry.'" But when he turned around, no one was there.

The lower terminal level of the Hell's Gate Airtram complex
is where most of the paranormal activity occurs.
COURTESY OF DIANE BELYK

What struck Brian was that Peter was a down-to-earth kind of person. "He doesn't elaborate, he doesn't embellish; he's a straight shooter."[16]

Another incident occurred about a year later. Operations manager Ken Green works throughout the year for the airtram company, and because his job often requires working at odd hours, he is sometimes the only person on the lower level where the workshop is located.

Ken had been working by himself, and in the late afternoon he made ready to finish for the day. As he stepped out into the cold, he could see that it would not be many minutes before the winter evening would give way to night. He walked toward the tram-loading dock where, looking down at the river, he could see low-lying fog obscuring the churning water far below. Even the thunder of the water striking the rocks was partially hushed by the fog.

Earlier, he had taken Tram 2 over from the upper level, and

now as he prepared to board it for the journey back, he was overcome by a feeling that something was wrong. Ken shivered involuntarily, but it was not from the cold. The hair on the back of his neck stood up. He looked across the dock to the space where Tram 1 would have stood had it been operating. As he looked, a small white shape resembling a cloud moved in his direction. Ken observed that "for a cloud to be intense enough or dense enough for you to see it in a four-foot area, to me that's weird because clouds are not normally that dense." [17] He quickly closed the gondola door and set his tram in motion away from whatever had been moving toward him.

Ken had another eerie experience, again when he was alone on the west side. Early one morning in 2011, he was in the workshop sanding some pieces of wood. Over the noise of the sander, he heard three loud distinctive knocks. Puzzled, he opened the door, but nothing was visible. Believing that it might have come from the CPR tracks, he checked the area, but no railway service vehicle could be seen.

A few minutes after he had returned to his job, he again heard the knock, knock, knock sounds. There was something disturbing about them. The strikes were heavy, like the creepy raps upon a door heard in so many horror movies. Under the circumstances, Ken considered it was time to postpone the workshop project until later.

Not all paranormal phenomena near the terminal dock take place during the off-season. One particularly malevolent ghost, called Edward, has been encountered under a remote area of the gold-panning deck. Although he is never seen, the phantom makes his presence known. After walking over this area, visitors and workers report sudden upset stomachs combined with feelings of oppression. When the people move away, the sensations rapidly disappear.

For many years, stories have circulated about a slight Asian man, dressed in a black coat and trousers, seen in the area. In late May of 2011, a new employee, Clare Neri, saw what she described as a "little Asian boy" on the stairs leading from the patio deck. Clare was standing on the deck watching the figure. Believing that the boy was a living person, she turned the corner leading to the stairs to talk to him. But to her amazement, in the short time he was out of sight, the little fellow had vanished. "I was shocked," Clare recalled. "I thought, where did he go?"[18] At the time she had not heard the story of the little Asian man who was said to haunt that area, so she had no idea that the "boy" was a ghost.

The attractions on the lower level are also the scene of many disconcerting happenings. On a warm summer day in 2009, Gina Davidson was employed at the Fudge Factory. While she was working at the sink, she was suddenly aware of cool air upon her. At first believing that someone had opened the door, she thought, "That was a nice breeze that came through."[19] But then she realized the door was too far away to create the effect. Although at the time she would not have been aware of this, the "breeze" probably was similar to the shafts of cold air commonly reported in haunted buildings. For witnesses, such occurrences are often accompanied on an unconscious level by the feeling that something unnatural is taking place, which would account for why Gina continues to remember the event long after it occurred.

One year earlier, Gina's co-worker at the Fudge Factory was witness to a strange event. She was working in the shop when a brick of candy dislodged itself from the top shelf. Instead of falling straight down according to the laws of physics, it arced from the counter to land in the middle of the floor. Gina, who did not have the same view of the event, caught sight of the fudge as it landed.

The Fudge Factory is not the location for most of the haunted activity at the complex—that distinction belongs to the Gold Panner Gift Shop. Interestingly, the building was contractor Andrew Onderdonk's cookhouse during the construction of the rail line through the canyon, and probably served the same purpose later for the CPR crews who maintained the line. The story of Genevieve, or Genny, as she is affectionately called, has circulated among airtram employees for some time. One staff member is said to have even spoken with the soft-voiced young woman.[20]

Roberta, the retail manager of the Gold Panner Gift Shop, has not been easily influenced by the stories of the haunted store. Nevertheless, she has had some peculiar experiences while working in the building. Roberta is first on the premises early in the morning and has heard the creaks and groans within the store. Always, though, she has put them down to the age of the building. Yet other events have been more difficult to explain.

One morning in 2009, Roberta was in her office at eight-thirty in the morning when she heard people talking on the walkway outside the building. "The voices sounded like women," Roberta recalled, "but I couldn't hear what they were saying."[21] Believing that the speakers were other managers who had arrived early and were chatting, she went back to her work. After a few minutes, when the conversation continued, Roberta thought she would go outside to say hello. However, when she opened the door, there were no people standing there. Indeed, no one was in sight.

Sometimes the smallest incidents appear to be singularly perplexing. In 2010, Roberta was sitting at the cash register in the gift shop. Suddenly she heard a crash near where she was sitting. Thinking something had fallen off the shelf, she searched the area, but nothing was out of place. However, as she walked toward the rear of the store, she noticed the trash lid lying some distance from its container. "I took the lid and put it on, and I did everything I could to make it fall, but it wouldn't fall." It certainly was not the kind of top that would easily become displaced.

Incidentally, a year earlier Roberta had had another odd experience. She had to make a trip to the administration office in a building a short distance from the gift shop. The office shares a stairway with the fisheries exhibit and, as she began walking up the stairs, she was struck by the strong smell of cigarette smoke. Roberta does not smoke and is sensitive to the odour of tobacco.

The entire airtram site is a non-smoking facility, so no one should have been smoking, especially near such a public place as the fisheries exhibit. She looked for the offender, but no one was in sight. As she reached the top landing, the smell was gone. Surprised, she returned down the stairs. Again she encountered the smell of cigarette tobacco. Why the odour was so strong, and limited to the relatively open area of the lower stairs where it was more likely to dissipate, was hard to explain. After repeating the experiment several times, she was finally unable to smell the noxious odour anymore.

In 2008, Diane Watson was working in the storage area of the gift shop. One day, her task was to fold items from a new shipment of jackets and put them on the shelves. To make her job easier she had a wheeled cart and a folding board, which sped up the task of layering the jackets. After placing a neatly folded article on a shelf, she would take another jacket from the pile and layer it on the cart with the aid of the board. After she had folded five or six jackets, however, something inexplicable happened. To her surprise, when she returned to the cart, the folding board was gone. "All I had done," Diane said, "was to turn around, take two steps, get a jacket and then take two steps back [to the cart], but the board wasn't there at all."[22]

What could have happened? Then Diane remembered the stories about the haunted building. "The hair went up on the back of my neck, and I went running into the gift shop." According to her workmates, she was so shaken that the colour had drained from her face.

A fellow employee went to the storage area and searched for the missing object, but returned empty-handed. It was only later, when Donna, Diane's supervisor, made an exhaustive search of the storage area that the board was recovered. It was on a pallet, under a pile of T-shirts, about eight metres from Diane's cart. Incredibly, the board had been hidden at the opposite end of the room, far from where Diane had been working. Whether this mischievous ghost was Genny or some other visitor from beyond the grave is impossible to know.

As it is the most haunted building in the airtram complex, the gift shop was chosen, in the spring of 2011, when five of the new seasonal employees asked permission to stay overnight at the lower level. For the young people, staying in the haunted gift shop seemed to offer an exciting sleepover. As evening fell, they made themselves comfortable in the old building and chatted under a light supplied by a generator. When they were ready for sleep, one member of the group switched off the power. The engine sputtered to a stop, but the light did not go out, nor did the room darken. Even without power, as Andrew Naylor, an employee who was there at the time, recalled, "that one light was still on."[23] Perhaps it was a message to the new employees that the stories of the ghosts of Hell's Gate were very real.

The ghosts that have been seen and heard are only a few of the legion of phantoms that some say are drawn to the complex. Possibly because the airtram site has a festive atmosphere, most of the ghosts that seek out human company are benign.

Ferintosh Manor is haunted by Emily and the Dark Man.
COURTESY OF DIANE BELYK

CHAPTER TWO

HAUNTED HOSTELRIES

FERINTOSH MANOR

It was said in the village that Ferintosh Manor was haunted, but in 2001, when Burt Heacock and his partner, Barrie Fletcher, moved into their newly purchased bed and breakfast, they had never heard the rumours. It did not take them long to discover that their residence in Ferintosh, Alberta, 115 kilometres south of Edmonton, had at least two phantom guests.

There is a dark shade, a male who inhabits the partners' apartment in the basement, the stairs, and the hallway leading to the main floor kitchen. The other resident, who is more active, is a female ghost they have called Emily. She appears to confine her activities to above the basement level. Unlike the Dark Man, who can be a very noisy ghost and seems to enjoy frightening Burt and Barrie, Emily is generally a benign presence. Yet, as sometimes happens during hauntings, ghosts do not always behave as expected.

The house has an interesting history, and had it not been located in an isolated community, it would have fallen to the wrecker decades ago. In 1933, Reverend Victor Lindgren built his two-storey house not far from the shores of Little Beaver Lake. The home was an outstanding example of late four-square architecture, with its practical box shape, large upper balcony, and commodious front porch that provided plenty of shade during the warm days of summer. His new house was much too large for the minister's small family—he had another use for it.

In the winter of 1934, Reverend Lindgren began the Alberta Bible Institute. Its purpose was to educate students in the theology of the Church of God. Classes were taught in the Lindgren home, and a few live-in students were probably accommodated there as well. However, when the Canadian National rail service to Ferintosh was discontinued, students had no easy access to the bible college, and it was moved in 1936 to the town of Camrose, Alberta, thirty-eight kilometres away. The minister did not move to Camrose, but continued to preach in his Ferintosh tabernacle until 1948. After that year, the history of the house is not entirely clear until it came into the possession of the Campbell family in the 1950s.

The house, like many built in the Great Depression era, had a foundation of stone rather than concrete. Although Reverend Lindgren saved money at the time by having a stone foundation, in the long term it was a disaster. The porous stone allowed water to seep into the basement and rot the wooden supports. Finally, as the odour of mould and mildew increased, the residents could no longer tolerate the stench, and in the early 1960s the big house was boarded up and abandoned. The water level eventually rose so high that ducks treated the grounds as a pond.

As is common with long-vacant houses, it gained an unsavoury reputation within the community. The first inkling that the house was haunted probably happened while the home was still occupied. Two boys were planning to take their small boat onto Little Beaver Lake, and as they prepared to launch their frail craft, they happened to look up at the balcony above the lakeshore house. There they saw two ghosts, apparently twin boys, warning them to stay off the water. Many of the details of this story have been lost in time, but the warning probably came in advance of a fast-moving prairie storm that would have sunk their boat.[1]

During the time the house was abandoned, a number of Ferintosh children and teenagers succeeded in breaking in by prying loose one of the boards covering the windows. Two boys, who are now adults and are still residents of Ferintosh, decided to explore the house. When they reached the stairs leading to the attic loft, an ironing board crashed down the steps before them. They took this as a hint that they had over-stayed their welcome—if indeed they were ever welcome at all.

On another occasion, a teenaged girl and her friends bravely decided to take a Ouija board into the house to talk to the ghost or ghosts, and held their session in the empty dining room. They stretched out on the dusty hardwood floor with the board positioned in the centre of the group. Then the boys and girls placed two fingers lightly on the planchette. Soon its tip began to move on the letters at the top of the board until it spelled two words: GET OUT. The frightened teenagers needed no more encouragement—they quickly left.

After remaining deserted for thirty-two years, the house was bought and passed through the hands of a number of owners. During this period, the structure was raised and a concrete foundation poured under it. The rotting wood in the basement was replaced, and the house was partially restored to its original appearance. Finally, the previous owners turned the house into a bed and breakfast, which Barrie and Burt purchased.

The Dark Man and the Haunted Basement

Before moving into Ferintosh Manor, Burt and Barrie brought Spanky, their light grey Himalayan cat, there so that he could explore his new basement home. Spanky cautiously made his way through the dining room, and when he reached the basement kitchen, he looked up the stairs toward the back hall. "Spanky went absolutely berserk; he just hissed," Burt recalled. "His fur went up and he turned around and ran into a door in our kitchen cupboards."[2] He hid behind some packing boxes, and it was three days before Burt and Barrie could coax him from his retreat. Even then, when Burt tried to pick Spanky up, he resisted and scratched his owner, something the big cat had never done before.

Prior to taking possession of the house, Burt and Barrie felt there was something creepy about the hall that opened from their apartment to the first floor of the bed and breakfast. In an attempt to relieve the depressing weight that seems to hang over the hall, Burt painted it a different colour three times. The area is not open to guests, because it leads to the basement suite where they live, but different visitors to the apartment, each unaware the house is haunted, have mentioned that there is something eerie about this hallway.

After Spanky's traumatic introduction to his new home, he continued to avoid the hall. Several dogs that Barrie and Burt have owned through the years also have avoided it. Milo, their Great Pyrenees, would look up the hall as though he were aware that something was there—something no human could see.

Not all their pets' strange behaviour relates to the hall. Barrie and Burt have no doubt that a dark presence resides in their basement apartment. In 2006, they also had a Welsh corgi named Bailey. The dog was obtained from his original owners "on approval" because he could not be house-trained. Barrie and Burt attempted to solve the problem, but without success—the dog continued to soil their carpets.

The night before Bailey was to be returned to his original owner, he had been lying in his dog bed when he stood up abruptly and walked to the doorway to the bedroom. His fur stood on end, and for a little dog like a corgi, he emitted a most fearsome growl. He turned around three times, all the while issuing the threatening sound, and then entered the kitchen and drank from his water bowl. Then he returned and lay on his bed, but for hours he did not take his eyes off the doorway. "They always say," Barrie observed, "that animals see things we don't see."[3]

Over the years, Burt has frequently glimpsed a dark shadow moving in the suite. It appears to be a silhouette in human shape, but it usually disappears quickly. Barrie, also, experienced the shadow figure. The clock above the television displayed exactly two o'clock when, one morning in 2006, Barrie awoke to see a dark shadow in the doorway silhouetted against the dim light coming from the bathroom. It was the size and shape of a man and seemed to have something in its hand, like a cup of coffee. At first he thought it was his partner who had gone to the kitchen in the early hours to get something to drink. Barrie looked at the figure and said, "What are you doing?"

As the shape turned toward Barrie, he thought, "Oh shoot that's not Burt!"[4] Almost immediately the figure disappeared.

The next night, Barrie awoke again at exactly two o'clock in the morning to find the same figure in the doorway. As before, once Barrie was aware of its presence, the apparition quickly disappeared.

Burt and Barrie have not been the only witnesses to the Dark Man. On an evening when Barrie was away, one of their neighbours, a skeptic, visited Burt. As the neighbour sat, Burt noticed that he looked puzzled. The visitor asked, "Do you have anyone else here?"

"No. Why?"

"Well, I just saw a man's shadow go across your wall."[5]

The event did not change the man's view on ghosts, but a bizarre occurrence would later make him a believer.

Even for a very active haunting like at Ferintosh Manor, some episodes are strange. The brief presence of a third and very active spectre is a disturbing and frightening example. When the partners moved into the bed and breakfast, the basement suite had not been properly finished, so they hired a contractor to complete the job. One day Burt was with their dog, Milo, in the basement dining room, when he saw something move past their office door. "It was huge—it was a big white formation," he said. It seemed to be of cloudy, vaporous material, although it was not dense enough to prevent Burt from seeing through it. He had seen human shapes in the basement before, but never like this. "I just remember thinking, what the . . . ?" he said.

At the time, Marshall, their contractor, was in the bathroom repairing the ceiling. It was about eight o'clock in the evening when Burt left the dining room, entered the office, and, after a few minutes, went into the bedroom. "All of a sudden there was a loud crash and we both ran into the living room," Burt said. The room looked as if a fight had taken place there. A heavy chair was flipped over. "I looked down at the big black wing chair, and the wing was broken. The ottoman was thrown almost clear across the room. It was upside down and had evidently hit the television."

Against another wall, two heavy, wrought-iron CD stands had been turned over, and the plastic cases and shiny disks scattered across the floor. The incident had taken place in one or two seconds, but the chair and ottoman had been at the opposite end of the room to the CD stands. Even if it had been possible for living people to enter the room, they could not have inflicted so much damage in so short a time. Furthermore, Milo certainly would have given a warning bark. Earlier that day, the dog had seemingly been aware that something was wrong. During the six months Marshall had worked on their basement, the contractor had become familiar with the dog's habits. On this day, Milo seemed tense and would not settle in his bed. At times, he padded restlessly around the suite.

While apparitions are not common occurrences in most hauntings—sounds are often the only event—Ferintosh Manor is unusual in that so many sightings have been reported. "We've been here with friends," Burt said, "and twice we've had balls of light go flying through the basement living room and right through the wall." On July 2, 2011, Burt witnessed another translucent white shape pass the office door in their basement suite. It was much smaller than the shape he had witnessed during the renovations to the basement, but it was a much brighter white light.

Sounds, too, are frequently heard in the basement. Poltergeist-like phenomena are often associated with an active haunting, and this is the case with Ferintosh Manor.

Sometime in about 2008, Burt was sitting alone in the basement watching television, when he heard a tremendous crash from the kitchen. It was so loud it sounded as if the refrigerator had fallen over. "I jumped out of my chair and I came running over and there was nothing wrong anywhere. I even went outside, I looked at all the windows, I thought earthquake, but I could find nothing."

In 2009, one of the weirdest occurrences took place when several of the neighbours were visiting, sitting in Burt and Barrie's suite. "All of a sudden this strange doorbell noise sounded as if it were coming out of the floor," Barrie said. "We were all looking at each other."[6] Someone asked if they had bought a new doorbell.

Dumbfounded, Barrie and Burt replied in the negative. It was impossible to ring from where the sound came from, for it was under a cement floor. One of their visitors was the earlier skeptic, who insisted they must have purchased a new doorbell. Burt ran upstairs and pressed the front and back bells. Although they rang in their suite downstairs, they sounded nothing like the chimes they had just heard. During the evening the phantom chimes sounded on two more occasions. Not surprisingly, Burt observed, "Now the guy's a believer."[7]

Another inexplicable noise occurred several years after Barrie and Burt bought Ferintosh Manor. One Saturday, they were sitting in their suite when they heard what sounded like beads from a broken necklace striking the floor. It was as if they were falling from a height, bouncing and rolling across a wooden floor. The noise seemed to be coming from the guest room upstairs. Their first response was to laugh, but then they realized someone might have broken into the house. To frighten the intruder, Barrie and Burt called out loudly that they were armed and that they were coming up stairs. However, no intruder could be found, and no beads were scattered on the floor of the room.

On November 30, 2012, Burt and Barrie were in their living room when they heard "a lot of crashing and banging" coming again from the kitchen. When they went to investigate, nothing had been disturbed.

One of the most frightening events in the entire array of ghostly happenings is the sound of disembodied voices. A witness once described the experience as "like listening just beyond the Gates of Hell." Burt and Barrie have each experienced these ghostly sounds.

Before the basement renovations were completed, Burt was sitting in their suite when he became aware of something strange occurring.

All of these voices were coming out of one corner [of the living room]. Just a whole lot of voices talking at one time. I couldn't get the accent; I couldn't get what they were saying. There was no music—it was almost like a bar where everybody's talking at the same time but you can't understand what they're saying. It was scary. I walked into the bedroom thinking the voices might follow me and they didn't.

Typically, the babble of voices that is never quite close enough to be understood both terrifies and frustrates the listener. Later, Barrie was in the basement living room and he also heard voices coming from the corner. He too was unable to understand what they were saying.

Unusual odours, rather than a perfume, which is far more common in the bed and breakfast, have been part of the haunting of Barrie and Burt's suite. In 2008, their apartment was damaged by sewer backup and the representative from the restoration company and the insurance adjuster were standing together, estimating the cost of the required repairs. The adjuster was wearing open-toed sandals and was deeply engaged in conversation when she screamed and threw her hand over her face. "Oh my gosh, somebody has just sprayed my feet."

There was a not unpleasant masculine scent that she had never smelled before. Burt explained to her that this was the work of the ghosts who haunted Ferintosh Manor. Eventually she calmed down. Then suddenly she again felt the cold spray on her feet. "I'm a believer, I'm a believer," she screamed.[8]

Emily and the Haunted Bed and Breakfast

Emily, unlike the Dark Man, usually remains in the bed and breakfast. She is most active on the second floor, where three of the five guest rooms are located. She also occasionally visits the main floor, where her presence is felt most often in the kitchen.

Several years ago, a well-known psychic from Calgary was staying with her friend in Ferintosh. During her time there, she visited Burt and Barrie and told them that the ghosts who haunt the manor are a man and a woman. The male, she said, stays in the basement and is angered by all the noise created by the renovations that were continuing at the time. The female remains upstairs, is the dominant presence, and is usually able to keep the male shade under control because he can become irritable at times.

Burt believes that Emily has attached herself to the 1930s-era stove in the kitchen. The partners have a picture of a woman with long white hair near the appliance. One afternoon in about 2002, a couple arrived on the front porch. The man introduced himself as Gus and said he lived in Camrose. They had heard about the new bed and breakfast and asked whether it would be possible to have a tour if there were no other guests? Burt readily agreed and took them through the main floor bedrooms. As Gus walked across the hall, he turned in the direction of the kitchen and said, "Excuse me, but you have company." Surprised, Burt could only reply that, it being a weekday, there were no guests.

"But," Gus said, "she was standing right there."

"Where?" Burt asked.

"In the kitchen."

When the three people reached the kitchen, there was no one in the room.

"But," Gus said incredulously, "she was standing right there!"

"Who?" Burt said.

"A lady," the man replied. "She had long white hair and was wearing a long white dress."[9]

During her tour of the manor, the psychic described seeing the female ghost as a smiling older woman wearing a long white dress, sitting in a chair in the upstairs hall. Although the ghost was said to be "happy," she often takes a dislike to skeptics.

Early on, eerie sounds certainly had their effect on one non-believer. In 2001, when Burt and Barrie were not yet open for business, they had heard stories from their neighbours that the bed and breakfast was haunted. Among their friends, it was no secret that Burt and Barrie had bought a house that supposedly came complete with ghosts.

As they were arranging the furniture before receiving their first paying guests, two of their friends, Bill and Bruce, drove from Calgary to see the house. Bruce and Bill, when they arrived at the rear driveway, did not have a good view of the house. When Barrie and Burt walked with their friends to see the front of the property, Bruce exclaimed, "Oh my gosh, the house from *The Amityville Horror!*" Although it looks nothing like the Dutch Colonial dwelling that served as the setting for the frightening 1979 film, the severe architectural features of Ferintosh Manor certainly can bring to mind the typical "haunted house" of Hollywood movies.

Later, on a summer weekend, when Burt and Barrie had no other bookings, Bruce and Bill arrived from Calgary. Barrie had earlier bought a DVD of the movie *The Amityville Horror*, which they had intended to watch that evening. The friends arrived late Friday night after driving the 260 kilometres from Calgary. Bruce had worked all day and was fatigued after the long trip, so during the movie, he said he was too tired to stay up any longer. They paused the film, and Barrie showed him to the Twins Room (the five guest rooms retain the names given to them by the former owners) on the second floor where he would be sleeping.

Barrie later recalled, "Myself, Bill, and Burt were just talking before beginning the movie again when we saw Bruce standing in the doorway. I said, 'Oh, you changed your mind?'"

"Yeah," Bruce replied.

Bill looked at him quizzically, and asked, "Are you okay?"

Bruce did not answer, but asked, "Did anyone come upstairs for anything?"

Everyone shook their heads and asked why Bruce wanted to know.

"As I was getting ready for bed, I could hear somebody walking down the hallway upstairs. So I went out in the hall and nobody was there. I thought it was Bill playing a joke."[10] Shrugging off the experience, he had returned to the room when he heard the sound of footsteps on the stairs. He entered the hall in time to hear measured steps walking toward him, but he could see no one. Waiting no longer, he rushed down the stairs to join the others in the basement.

The next day while Burt, Barrie, and Bill took a walk down to the picturesque lake not far from the manor, Bruce, who had a sore foot, remained behind. When they returned, he explained that he heard a sound as if someone was banging on the wall behind him. It was in the summer, so the heating pipes could not have made the noise. Emily was apparently attempting to change the mind of a skeptic. Indeed, Bruce was later forced to concede, "There's some weird stuff going on in that house!"[11]

One of the times Emily showed her displeasure with a guest was after a man who considered himself an expert on bed and breakfasts contacted Burt. The man lived quite close to Ferintosh, and one day he stopped by the manor for coffee. Burt began by giving him a tour of the grounds, during which the visitor was critical of the gardens and offered ridiculous suggestions for what he regarded as "improving" the landscaping. The interior fared no better—the man criticized the decor. All the time he was present, he never stopped complaining about one room or another. The partners had spent many hours developing the gardens and painstakingly decorating the interior of the house in keeping with the 1930s style, and the man's comments displayed his ignorance of the subject. Burt could not wait for the obnoxious individual to leave.

Several months later Burt was surprised when the man phoned to book a double room for himself and his wife. They were assigned the Bridal Suite, and on the afternoon of their arrival, the man said he wanted to go up to his room to take a nap. After a while he came downstairs and, placing his hands on his hips, demanded to be told if the manor had ghosts. Burt and Barrie admitted that it was haunted and asked him why he wanted to know.

Their guest said, "I was asleep when suddenly I was aware that something was staring down at me. And there was a woman hanging over me in the bed and scowling at me. She had the meanest look."

"What did she look like?" Burt asked.

"She had long white hair."

"Did she have a white dress?"

"Yes, and then she just disappeared."[12]

After the couple left, Burt said to Barrie, "Emily thinks he's a big ass, too."

Emily's signature is a scent described as something like lavender perfume. At times it can be overpowering and can actually be seen hanging in the air as if it were sprayed by an atomizer. On one occasion, as Burt recalled:

> I wouldn't say she does it on command but once when we had some people and they were talking about [Emily], and I said sometimes she'll spray the perfume. And I said, 'Quick, over here, over here!' And they were amazed. There it was, the perfume. It was wet . . . a mist.[13]

Several years ago, a group of "scrapbookers" met at Ferintosh Manor. A woman and her daughter, who had taken the Bridal Suite, were the last to arrive. Burt was in the kitchen preparing dinner and noticed the voices of his guests coming from the living room. Although their conversation could not be heard clearly, he could make out the word "perfume," said repeatedly. Burt had some idea what their discussion was about and joined them.

"You're talking about perfume in your room?" he said to the older woman occupying the Bridal Suite.

"Yes" came the surprised response. "We walked in and there was this wet mist hanging in the air."

She had been questioning the other scrapbookers to see if they had been playing a joke on her and her daughter. Burt told them that a harmless ghost who sometimes makes her presence known by spraying perfume around the house haunts the manor. Emily's scent, when it is not overwhelming, occurs so often that Burt and Barrie are not aware of it until someone calls attention to it.

As was mentioned earlier, not all the odours smell like perfume. One year, a family booked several rooms at the manor. During the warm summer afternoon, while everyone else was enjoying the cool shade of the porch, one of the guests decided to nap in the Lindgren Room, on the main floor. After a short time he called Burt and Barrie to come to his room.

He was clearly excited about something. "Do you smell this?" he exclaimed.

Burt and Barrie shook their heads.

"Up here," he said pointing near the head of the bed.[14]

When Burt and Barrie approached the spot, they could smell the strong scent of cloves. Odours that are manifested in the manor seemingly arise from nowhere, and then disappear as quickly as they come.

In 2008, a technician from a satellite dish operator wired the guest rooms for television. After completing the job, as he was standing beside Burt on the back porch preparing the bill, the two men were overwhelmed by a familiar smell, as if someone had broken a jar of preserved peaches next to where they were standing. It lasted only a short time and was replaced by a masculine scent similar to Old Spice aftershave. These odd smells remain a puzzle, for they are not like Emily's scent.

One of the most frightening incidents during a haunting is to hear the name of a person being called by an unseen entity. Yet Emily often seems to exude a feeling of calm rather than terror. One year Ferintosh Manor hosted a group of hunters who were after big game. One of the guides, a woman, was given the Bridal Suite on the second floor. When, late in the day she had a chance to be alone with Burt, she asked, "Do you have ghosts?"

When Burt asked her why, she said that in the middle of the night she was awoken by a female voice softly calling her name, "Cathleen." At first she was frightened and sat upright in bed. "But," Burt said, "it called her name again, and she felt a real peace and she was easy with it."[15]

While many of the events take place in daylight or when a light is on, one terrifying episode occurred in 2007 when several friends bought two of their group a weekend stay at Ferintosh Manor as an anniversary gift. To help the husband and wife celebrate, their friends also booked rooms. The couple was given Kenny's Room, which has two double beds. During the evening Burt and the couple, along with their friends, sat in the kitchen talking until eventually the husband grew tired and went to their room.

After a short time, his wife also decided to retire. Because her husband is a light sleeper and, once disturbed, has difficulty falling asleep again, she decided to use the room's unoccupied bed. She undressed and prepared for sleep, but the room was very dark so she cracked the door to the hall open before slipping under the covers. A thin shaft of light shone in from the space between the door and the frame, but it did little to overcome the darkness.

She was still awake when she was suddenly aware that someone was sitting on the corner of her bed. The feeling was unmistakable—it was as if a body were pressing down on the mattress. It was so dark that nothing could be seen, but her first thought was that her husband had awoken and was now at the foot of the bed. She sat up and put her hand out to her husband, but she did not touch him. Instead she felt the grasp of icy fingers over her hand. Quickly she drew away; as she did so the weight lifted from the bed and something seemed to sweep rapidly across the room until it briefly obstructed the light that filtered in from the hall. Then the door clicked shut and the room was black as night.

Burt and Barrie were in their suite one night when they heard noises coming from what sounded like the Twins Room on the second floor.

Barrie shut off the television and asked, "Did you hear that?"[16] Burt had. Barrie's first thought was of Milo, the dog, but Milo was downstairs with them. The sound resembled a person moving noisily about the room. When they investigated, nothing could be found.

As was mentioned earlier in this book, ghosts frequently make use of a building's electrical wiring system or electronic components to make their presence known. This has also happened in Ferintosh Manor. One Christmas season, when Barrie and Burt were hosting a party at the manor, they had wrapped garlands and lights around the banister and plugged in the electrical cord. The coloured bulbs on the banister were on, but the effect was lost in the bright room. "Turn off the lights so we can see what it looks like," Burt suggested. Barrie had not had time to take a step toward the switch when the overhead lights went off. "Thank you, Emily," said Burt.

On another occasion Burt was removing some items from the porch and, as he walked by one of the bedrooms, he noticed that the bedside lamp was on. He made a mental note to turn it off when he finished, but the next time he walked by, he heard the distinctive click of the lamp switch and the light went out. No one was in the room. At Ferintosh Manor, the click of a switch as the light is turned on or off in a vacant room is not an isolated event.

In 2008, a former guest returned with five friends. Well aware that the manor was haunted, she asked Burt if they could have a tour of his haunted basement apartment. Burt and the six women went through the suite until they reached the kitchen, where the previous guest said, "Tell them about the lights."

"What lights?"

"Tell them how your ghost turns the lights on and off."[17]

She had just finished speaking when the ceiling light went on. Yet as Burt said, "The switch [for the light] is way over on the other side of the kitchen." It did not stop there: "Then the lights on the underside of the cabinets, on a separate switch, came on." The guests had a frightening demonstration of the haunted suite.

One amusing incident concerned an ornament on a cabinet on the main floor—a music box that played the melody from the 1952 hit song "I Saw Mommy Kissing Santa Claus." On top of the box were the figures of Santa and a woman twirling around while the melody played. Even if the mechanism had not been rewound, the box often began to play when Burt or

Barrie walked by the cabinet. Whenever the music box began playing, Burt had the habit of acknowledging the ghost's presence. On one occasion, he said, "Hi, Emily." As he walked toward the closet to take out a shirt, he heard a click as the ceiling light above him went on. In her own way, Emily was evidently acknowledging the greeting.

The Dark Man appears to enjoy late-night television. Barry will sometimes turn off the television in the basement suite, place the remote control on the mantel, and go to bed, only to enter the living room the next morning and find the television on. Yet, within haunted Ferintosh Manor, where so many unexplainable activities have occurred over the years, the strange behaviour of the electronics remains just a minor puzzle.

An event that can only be described as bizarre occurred several years ago when Burt and Barrie walked into the main floor kitchen to discover the yellow plaid curtains lying on the floor. "The curtain rod was still in place and the curtain was a slide-through," Burt said. Shortly after the partners opened Ferintosh Manor, they had a similar experience in the guest living room. Burt and Barrie entered the room one morning to find the cushions from the sofa scattered over the floor.

On another occasion, several people walking past the bed and breakfast during the off-season, when they knew the partners were away, saw a woman standing in one of the windows on the main floor. What they described as particularly creepy was that the female figure followed them from window to window as they walked past the house. Because they were familiar with the story of Emily, they were interested. They walked back and forth in front of the house to see what would happen, and Emily continued to follow them. It was as if she were protecting the house during one of the few times no one was in the manor.

As with most hauntings, it is impossible to neatly categorize the many occurrences at Ferintosh Manor. While concluding that only two ghosts haunt it—the Dark Man in the basement suite and Emily in the bed and breakfast—would be easy, doing so would be incorrect. Who, for example, are the two white apparitions that have been seen in Burt and Barrie's suite?

Another "loose end" happened when three neighbourhood teenagers dropped over to watch satellite television. According to Thomas, one of the young people present, "Me, my sister, and a friend were standing at the top of the stairs [leading to the basement suite]. My friend and I looked down and we saw just legs and a white dress walking across [the basement living room]. I walked downstairs and I didn't see anything."[18] Was this Emily in the basement? Her apparition has never been seen in Burt and Barrie's suite, and furthermore, because her legs were visible, her dress was shorter than other witnesses have described it.

Over the years, the activity at the bed and breakfast tends to be cyclic. As of November 2012, with the odd exception, the ghosts of Ferintosh Manor have been quiet for some time. Yet, given the extensive haunted history of the house, it seems safe to conclude that Emily, the Dark Man, or whatever else is occasionally witnessed there will not remain at rest for long.

COBBLESTONE MANOR: A WORK UNFINISHED

Whenever Ivan and Marsha Negrych visited Cardston, Alberta, 230 kilometres south of Calgary, they stopped to enjoy an excellent meal at the unique restaurant in Cobblestone Manor. As a business opportunity, the restaurant appealed to them, and in 2002 the couple made the decision to buy it. One of the outstanding features of the mansion was the exquisite craftsmanship of the structure; it had been created single-handedly by its builder, Henry Hoet. However, little did Ivan and Marsha know when they bought the beautiful building that even in death, Henry would remain bound to his life's passion.

The building of Cobblestone Manor is a fascinating story, and one that has been told elsewhere.[19] Yet to understand the haunting of this beautiful bed and breakfast and restaurant, it is necessary to know something about the man who built it, stone by stone.

Today, mature trees and shrubs surround the sprawling, two-storey building, making appreciating its size difficult. Much larger than it looks, the manor comprises more than 450 square metres, including a one-time carriage house that serves as the bed and breakfast.

The builder, Henry Hoet, an extremely talented crafts-man, was born in Belgium and immigrated to Canada via the United States in 1911. At the time he was probably in his early thirties. Why he chose to live in the little community of Cardston remains unclear. It was certainly not to live among immigrants with a similar background: his Flemish roots and Catholic religion meant that he had nothing in common with the Mormon settlers who had arrived in Cardston from Utah in 1887.

Cardston residents saw the new arrival as a peculiar individual who preferred his own company. Henry's goal was not to make friends but to devote his life to constructing a mansion like nothing else ever seen in Alberta. It would be a monument to his singular obsession, yet the reason for its existence in this sparsely settled area would be lost forever in the labyrinth of Henry's mind.

His masterpiece had modest beginnings. About two years after arriving in Cardston, Henry purchased a log house near

Lee's Creek. Spring floods earlier in the century had damaged or destroyed most of the dwellings too close to the creek, but this one was high enough up the embankment to escape harm from the raging waters.

For Henry, his humble dwelling was only the first step in creating a residence that stood apart from any other home in Alberta. As a talented artisan, the Belgian immigrant was unrivalled. While the residents of Cardston saw only devastation where the floods had denuded the land of topsoil, Henry saw the boulders and sand that remained as the building material for his house. Henry used the existing cabin as a framework and moved boulders up the hill to create the exterior walls of what was the beginning of Cobblestone Manor.

Once the walls were completed, Henry began work on the interior. By training he was a cabinetmaker—a trade he apparently learned during his years in the United States—and the interior woodwork shows the superb skills of a master of his trade. Honeycomb inset ceilings and wood panelling, wood cabinets, and a beautiful staircase reflect Henry's ability. In the Golden Oak Room, which is now part of the restaurant's dining room, sixty-one pieces of mitred oak have been fitted meticulously into the ceiling. Amazingly, no nails were used in building the manor. Almost all of the money Henry earned working on construction jobs was spent on items like the beautiful oak panelling and tiffany lamps that adorn the manor today. The house had all the aristocratic pretensions of a small mansion in Henry's native Belgium.

When he was asked why he was building this magnificent house, Henry would mumble something about it being for his lover who would be joining him from his homeland, but he never received nor sent letters to Belgium. His reason for building the house had no simple explanation.

The ghost of Henry Hoet remains bound to his creation, Cobblestone Manor.
COURTESY OF DIANE BELYK

Over the years Henry's mental health declined and, by 1928, he was incapable of caring for himself. He experienced a complete break with reality; he was picked up by the police, placed in a straitjacket, and taken away to the mental hospital at Ponoka, Alberta. Henry's mental illness, diagnosed as general paralysis of the insane (now known as general paresis), was the result of untreated syphilis and included increasingly severe psychotic episodes. Finally, the destruction of the neural pathways in Henry's brain resulted in his death in 1949.

After his confinement, the house was put on the auction block for unpaid debts. Even in 1928 dollars, the amount that was received for the mansion and its contents was extremely small. Had it been built near a major city, it no doubt would have attracted a wealthy buyer, but Cardston was a small agricultural community out on the prairie.

The building came into the possession of a number of different owners until 1977, when Ed and Arlene Flickinger bought it; they operated it as a restaurant until 2002. In that year the present owners, Ivan and Marsha Negrych, purchased it and added a bed and breakfast operation to the existing business.

The manor was thought to be haunted. Cardston residents claim to occasionally see Henry's ghost inspecting his property and, not surprisingly, people avoided the house after dark. Given Henry's obsessive attachment to the mansion he built but never finished, it seems likely that he would have been drawn after death to his grandiose creation.

From the day they moved in, Ivan and Marsha Negrych were aware that there was something strange about the manor. The building had an eerie feeling about it.

If the odd events had taken place only occasionally, they could have been blamed on absent-mindedness. However, they happened much too regularly. Marsha first noticed them soon after the Negrychs' opened the manor for business, and these petty occurrences have continued until today. "Things will get moved in the house," she said. "You'll put a thing someplace and when you go to get them they're not there. Doors that have been locked are opened."[20]

Henry seems to have taken pleasure in frightening one of the cooks. To her horror she would often catch sight of a shadow standing in the doorway to the kitchen. She would be working alone when the microwave ovens would turn on by themselves.

At other times she would be washing pots and pans and, after leaving them to dry, she would hang them from the high hooked bar on the wall. As she placed one securely on the hook and turned to pick up another, there would be a terrific crash, and she would find the pot or pan she had just hung up on the floor. The hooks had been designed to securely hold the cooking implements by the holes in their handles. Therefore, the utensils could not easily slip off their hooks. Moreover, the pots and pans always fell when she was not looking in their direction. There was simply no logical explanation for what was happening. The harassed worker remained at the manor for less than two weeks before she quit.

At separate times, two of Ivan and Marsha's children have witnessed a shadowy figure in the family's living quarters on the upper floor. Although Ivan has never seen anything, he has heard the muted voices of a man and a woman. They are not arguing. Instead they are speaking very quietly as if they do not wish to wake anyone.

The family pet is aware of something as well. Usually between two and four o'clock in the morning the Negrychs' dog, Buddy, who slept on a little balcony area on the second floor, would begin to bark and stare into the house. "He's not barking outside," Marsha observed. "He's barking *inside* because he senses something."

Once, at about three o'clock in the morning, in 2004, Ivan's fourteen-year-old daughter woke him, whispering, "He's sitting in the restaurant."

"Who's sitting in the restaurant? It's early in the morning," Ivan answered sleepily.

"The ghost," the girl said, taking her father by the arm and leading him downstairs.

In the Golden Oak Room, she pointed to a rocking chair. "He's sitting there by the fireplace."

When her father seemed bewildered she looked surprised. "You can't see him?" she asked. "He's looking at you. He's all dressed in white and he's just sitting there."

"Where?" Ivan asked.

She walked over to the rocking chair and said, "Right here, right beside me."[21]

As it happened, the chair had been part of the original furnishings of Henry's house, and it apparently had been a favourite place for him to sit and relax after a busy day. There is a photo of Henry sitting in it, but it was unlikely then that Ivan's daughter knew of the picture.

Disembodied voices have been heard in Cobblestone
Manor's bed and breakfast in the old carriage house.
COURTESY OF DIANE BELYK

Other people have seen something strange on the lower
floor. On Sundays, when the restaurant is closed and the
Negrych family is at church, Cardston residents have seen
someone moving about in the restaurant. No one has had a
close look at this uninvited visitor, but Ivan feels it is almost
certainly Henry.

Spirits that have been heard on the second floor of
Cobblestone Manor also haunt the bed and breakfast, which
is a separate building. Phantom footsteps have been heard on
the stairs, and eerie sounds have interrupted the silence of
the night. One evening, two women from Edmonton booked
separate rooms at the bed and breakfast, which was otherwise
unoccupied. Their intention was to start out early the next day
to enjoy a few days of hiking, but when they failed to turn up
for breakfast in the morning, Ivan went upstairs to check. He
knocked on the women's doors, but received no response, so he

became concerned. When he opened the door he was surprised to see the money for the room on the table, with a note from the two women saying they had decided to leave very early.

Several weeks later, one of the women stopped by for lunch and explained the reason for their sudden departure. Alone on the second floor of the building, they had retired early to their rooms. About two o'clock in the morning, one of the women awoke and heard a male and a female voice talking outside her door, and then footsteps walking along the wooden floor of the hallway. There was something puzzling about the sounds, as though the voices arose from no living people. She called out to her friend in the next room and asked if she had the radio or television turned on. "No," her friend replied, but she had also heard the voices and footsteps.

What was apparently happening outside their doors could not be ignored. Yet, as soon as the first guest swung her legs over the side of the bed and put her feet on the floor, the noises stopped. When she lifted her feet again the sounds returned. After experimenting with this bizarre phenomenon several times, she walked across the floor and opened her door. The passageway was deserted. However, when she returned to bed, the phantom voices and the footsteps began again.

Though the words exchanged between the man and woman were subdued, as if they were speaking quietly together, the voices were terrifying nonetheless. It was obvious that the women were hearing the muted sounds of people who were surely long dead. About four o'clock the sounds stopped, and soon afterward the two women, shaken by what had occurred, decided to make an early start on their day. The identities of the ghosts that move freely between the two buildings remain a mystery.

Many investigators of the paranormal believe that one reason spirits stay earthbound is something they have left undone. For the ghost of Henry Hoet, it is Cobblestone Manor, his magnificent obsession that will remain forever a work unfinished.

THE HISTORIC BISHOPS RESIDENCE

"As the expression goes, I'm from Missouri," Les Shoemaker declared. "If I don't see it, I don't believe it."[22] The owner of the Historic Bishops Residence Bed and Breakfast can be described as a firm non-believer in ghosts, but the large, three-storey brick building, with its distinctive, rounded front porch, has long been said to be haunted. And it lives up to its reputation.

In the spring of 1906, Father Louis-Joseph-Pierre Gravel founded the French-speaking community of Gravelbourg on the banks of the Wood River in south-central Saskatchewan. More than simply a culturally isolated settlement in the new, predominantly English-speaking province, Gravelbourg was intended to be one of the centres for the maintenance and expansion of the Roman Catholic religion and the French language in the Canadian West. The community attained special prominence when the Church of St. Philomena (later Our Lady of the Assumption Co-Cathédrale), with its twin spires, became the spiritual centre of the newly created Gravelbourg diocese in 1930.

The Bishops Residence was begun in 1918 and completed in 1920 as a rectory for the church in Gravelbourg. In 1930, it became the home of the Bishop of the Diocese of Gravelbourg. Unlike the parish priest, the bishop, with his retinue of priest administrators and nuns who lived on the second and third floors, was not part of the community. He remained a remote figure.

As fewer men entered the priesthood and church attendance diminished, the Gravelbourg diocese was amalgamated with the Diocese of Regina in 1998, and the church became a co-cathedral without a residing bishop's chair. In 2008, the diocese sold the house to Les Shoemaker, who opened it as a bed and breakfast.

Latin- and French-speaking ghosts haunt the Historic
Bishops Residence in Gravelbourg, Saskatchewan.
COURTESY OF DIANE BELYK

Earlier, when the residence stood empty, it was whispered
in the community that the house was haunted. A nun was said
to have been seen standing at a third-storey window, but Les
thinks the nun's ghost was nothing more than the way the light
strikes that clouded windowpane.

In April 2009, he married his fiancée, Mely, whom he had
met during one of his visits to Mexico. Five of Mely's friends
from Mexico were staying on the third floor of the Bishops
Residence to attend the ceremony. Les recalled the morning
that they were to leave. "We went upstairs to make sure they
knew their times of departure. We found them all in the one
bedroom, room 305, with a chair in front of the door. They

were totally petrified because they swore there were ghosts in the hallway in the middle of the night."[23]

Les believes that other noises, such as the thumps and bumps that are sometimes heard in the night, are caused by the expansion and contraction of the pipes of the heating system. (It should be noted that the Shoemakers do not sleep in the Bishops Residence but instead occupy a trailer behind the main house. Thus, they may not experience the gamut of ghostly events that their guests do.)

Mely encountered the paranormal one evening after dinner, when she decided to take a bath in the washroom in the basement. Through the door she heard what she thought was Les's voice speaking French. She called out, asking him why he was trying to speak French when he did not know the language. She received no reply. When she went upstairs, she found Les asleep in front of the television. When she again asked him about his attempt to speak French, he denied it and went on to say he had not been in the basement at that time. Mely was concerned, for she was certain someone had broken into the house, but Les could find no evidence of forced entry.

Some of the guests also have had unusual experiences at the bed and breakfast. In the first months of 2011, a young Vietnamese woman was staying there while teaching at the French immersion school in Gravelbourg. She was convinced the house was haunted, for she would often return to her room to find her clothes and other personal items in disarray.

In early July 2011, an overnight guest was awakened by the sound of people speaking Latin. Although she did not understand what was said, she had attended Roman Catholic mass at a time when it was given in Latin, and she was familiar with the way the language sounded.

In late July 2011, two teenaged sisters, Tanica and Ashley

Drinkle, and their grandfather, Harvey Drinkle, arrived for the night before going on to Regina. They had been given rooms on the second floor. After their long drive, first Tanica, then Ashley, took a shower before climbing into bed to watch television. After watching the screen for more than an hour, they heard the unmistakable sound of the shower.

"I know I turned the shower off!" Ashley said.

"I know you did," Tanica assured her.[24]

The sound of water spraying in the stall continued for about five minutes and then stopped. It was just enough time for someone to have a quick shower.

"It was scary," Tanica said. It was even more so when she checked the next morning to find the shower tap was in the "off" position.

Only during breakfast did the sisters learn that the Bishops Residence was reputed to be haunted. Given the events of the previous night, it was not a surprise to them.

Even though no one claims to have seen the ghosts of the Bishops Residence, the phantoms have made their presences known. While it may be possible to explain away the nun at the window or the thumps and bumps in the night, too many other happenings are left unexplained.

L'AUBERGE CLÉMENCE

L'Auberge Clémence Inn on the Prairie is in the small bilingual community of Elie, Manitoba, fifty kilometres west of Winnipeg. This unusual bed and breakfast stands as a memorial to its seventy years as a convent. One of the reminders of the past is the spirit of at least one departed sister who continues to haunt the building.

For Jean Aquin, 1975 was a memorable year. After he and his wife, Linda, returned from their honeymoon, he discovered that he no longer had a job—the ambulance company in Winnipeg for which he worked had been taken over by the provincial government, and there was no place for him in the new organization. Renouncing the big city, Jean and Linda settled in Elie, his hometown, where he earned a meagre living performing odd jobs. One of the Aquins' nearest neighbours was the Sisters of Our Lady of the Missions, a teaching order at St. Martha's Convent in Elie. Two of Jean's aunts had been members of the order, and one had died tragically at age twenty-two of polio. Jean later obtained the job of mowing the lawn and tending the shrubs on the two hectares of land around the convent.

The mammoth, three-storey, 790-square-metre brick convent was completed in 1915 after a fire had completely destroyed the original building on New Year's Day, 1912. In the new convent, forty live-in students were housed in a single dormitory on the third floor.

Even after taking on a new job as a school bus driver, Jean continued to tend the convent property. However, with falling student attendance and fewer women willing to take the vows, the convent closed in the 1990s. The sisters leased the building as offices for a short time, but then it stood vacant for years. Vandals broke in and destroyed part of the interior, and young people used it for parties, inflicting further damage.

The windows of the Aquins' house looked out on the once-beautiful building, and Jean was dismayed to see it deteriorating. If it were left vacant and untended for much longer, he feared it would be torn down. He felt strangely drawn to the convent and did not want to see it destroyed.

Jean contacted the Sisters of Our Lady of the Missions and expressed his interest in buying the building and opening it as a bed and breakfast. Negotiations continued for four years—he could not afford the market price, but, as he told the sisters, if anyone else bought the convent, it would be for the value of the property, and the building would be torn down. He, however, would maintain the structure in keeping with its long tradition. At last the order was swayed by sentiment rather than monetary value, and Jean and Linda became the building's owners. With little money for renovations, the Aquins faced a daunting project. "This was 8,500 square feet," Jean recalled. "Everybody told us we were crazy—it was impossible to get it done. But the way things went it would get done."[25]

They began by gutting the third floor, where most of the guest rooms were to be located, and finishing one room at a time. While the project was still in progress, they had a college instructor book one of the completed rooms, even though work was continuing around him. Not long after this first guest moved in, more than a dozen members of a road crew asked to be billeted. The inflow of cash from these early guests meant the job could proceed much more quickly than Jean had expected. Jean and Linda were not alone; relatives also volunteered their time.

Many of the religious statues that had once adorned the convent and had been dispersed throughout the community were returned. After the five guest rooms had been completed, the chapel was renovated and a private, two-bedroom suite was created on the second floor. As well as the reconstructed kitchen, a tea room, dining room, parlour, and gift shop were added on the main floor.

Jean certainly feels that he was destined to save the beautiful old building from destruction. When they needed money to continue with their project, funds would amazingly be found. Jean had anticipated it would take five years to complete the renovations, but the job was done in six months. L'Auberge Clémence officially opened twelve days before Christmas in 2002.

L'Auberge Clémence. This former convent still has a ghostly sister in residence.
COURTESY OF DIANE BELYK

Almost from the beginning, Jean and Linda were aware that there was something peculiar going on in their new house. "As we were doing the renovations, things started happening," Jean said. One night he and his cousin, Ron, were working on the third floor. When they finished, they walked down the stairs until they reached the second-floor landing. The two men stopped suddenly. In the hallway leading to the chapel, Jean smelled rose perfume. He said to his cousin, "Do you smell that?"

"Yes," Ron answered. "It's pretty strong."

"Did you spill any perfume on the carpet up here, by any chance?" Jean called down to Linda who was working on the main floor with Ron's sister, Joyce.

"No," Linda answered. "We haven't been upstairs yet."

"This is weird," Jean said, "because it smells of perfume up here, and it's quite strong."

The two women joined the men on the second floor to investigate. Neither Linda nor Joyce had an explanation for the strong scent that permeated the hallway.

While Linda and Joyce remained on the second floor, Jean and Ron continued down the stairs. They became aware of the same smell on the main floor. As they later learned, the scent was no longer on the second floor. "When Ron and I came downstairs it followed us," Jean said. It hung in the air for about fifteen or twenty minutes before it dissipated. None of the convent sisters would have worn perfume, so its origin was a mystery.

Frequently, Jean hears footsteps passing near him. As he turns around to look, he catches only glimpses of someone. He never sees the face or the body, just someone wearing pants and shoes. The image is moving so fast it is only a blur. "Every time it happens, the hair on my arms stands up."

Ron once saw Jean's father's spirit in the main floor corridor. (Jean had told his father that he wanted to buy the building, but the older man died before the purchase went through.)

On one occasion Jean heard footsteps on the stairs. The sound continued halfway up the steps and then stopped abruptly. Thinking it was Linda, he asked her whether she had been walking on the stairs. "No," she replied, "I thought it was you." Jean searched the building to see if they had an intruder, but he could find no one.

Once, after they opened for business, Linda had another eerie experience. In early 2003, she was leaving the private suite on the second floor carrying an armful of blankets to be washed. The combination bedroom and sitting room has two doors— one leading to the second bedroom, the other to the chapel and staircase. Linda had a difficult time leaving, for her arms were full. Amazingly, both doors opened at the same time. It was as if the ghost were trying to help but did not know through which door Linda wanted to go.

Another odd occurrence that continued until recently involved the chimes that announced people arriving at the rear of the house. In the early hours—between two and three o'clock in the morning—the rear doorbell would often ring. Since the Aquins usually slept on the second floor, Jean would take the stairs and go through the kitchen to answer the door. At first they thought it was mischief-makers, but, as the bell continued to ring, he wondered why they did not become bored with the joke. Indeed, the perpetrators seemed too persistent. The noise did not depend on the weather or the season—summer or winter, whether the night was warm or cold, wet or dry, the chimes continued to disturb the household. Although the doorbell did not ring every night, it happened often enough to be very annoying.

Jean locked the outside door to the porch, which should have denied access to the doorbell. Yet the chimes continued to ring. He traced the wiring and could find nothing wrong with the circuit. The chime mechanism appeared to work perfectly, for the phantom ring occurred only during the early morning hours.

Finally, Jean sprinkled sand in the area around the bell button and waited for the chimes to ring again. When they did, he found in the morning that no impression was left in the soft sand. It confirmed what Jean had long suspected. The question was not *who*, but *what* was ringing the bell. Only when he cut the power to the rear doorbell were the early morning chimes at last silenced.

One of the sisters haunts the King Room, the largest bedroom on the third floor. The nun is never seen, but in an odd way she makes herself known. Not long after L'Auberge Clémence opened, a visitor from North Dakota booked the room. Over a period of about four months, he would arrive on Sunday night and leave on Thursday, and during this time Jean fell into easy conversation with the affable guest. After Oscar (not his real name) had spent about three weeks at the bed and breakfast, he was preparing to return home for his three-day stay. Before leaving he asked Jean if he knew that there was a nun "flying" around the third floor.

"What?" Jean asked, incredulously. The guest admitted the nun was not flying nor had he seen anything, but he was sure there was a ghost there nonetheless. When Jean asked him how he knew, Oscar said, "It's very simple. When I go to bed at night I close my door and when I wake up in the morning my door is wide open."

Jean attempted to explain that the hardware on the door had never been replaced and was very old. Further, the shaking of the ground as a result of passing freight trains probably caused the door to open. Oscar was not convinced. He was sure that it was the ghost of a nun who was visiting him. Jean offered to change the lock, but the guest said that it would not stop her from opening his door. Oscar did not seem to be bothered by the events, but Jean was sure there was a natural explanation for what was happening.

One Thursday after Oscar had left, a couple booked the private suite on the second floor where Jean and Linda usually slept. After preparing the suite, the Aquins moved into the room Oscar had vacated. While Linda went to bed earlier, Jean completed several kitchen chores before going upstairs about one o'clock in the morning. After changing for the night in the bathroom, "I closed the door to the King Room and I lay back on the bed," he said. Then, "I heard click,

click, click [and] I got up and turned on the light and the door was open."

He woke Linda and told her the door had just opened on its own. "No way," she said sleepily. Jean closed the door and tested the latch, but no matter how much he shook it and pulled on the door, it would not open. The only logical conclusion was that earlier, when he closed the door, the latch had not slipped into the striker plate correctly. This time, Jean made sure it was latched properly, and further, he pushed and turned the handle to lock it securely, then walked across the room and sat on the bed.

A moment later he heard click, click, click again and turned around to see the door swing open. Now the hair on Jean's arms stood up. "There was nothing wrong with the door, the hardware was fine. Somebody was opening that door," Jean said. Oscar was right; there was a spirit haunting the third floor.

Sometime later a young couple booked the King Room for the weekend, and during the last night of their stay they asked Jean to wake them up early the next day. However, the bed and breakfast had other guests and he was particularly busy. It was not until nine o'clock, when he saw them, that he remembered they had asked for an early call. At breakfast, the woman said, "By the way, Jean, did you come and wake us up this morning?"

"No," he admitted. "I forgot all about it."

"Oh," she said. "We were just wondering because we thought you had come upstairs and opened our door to call us, but didn't wake us because we were still asleep. And then you forgot to close our door."

"No," Jean said. "I didn't go upstairs."

"Then how come our door was open?"

Because he did not want to frighten his guests, Jean did not tell them that the King Room was haunted, so he bent the truth and said that sometimes an extra-long train would shake the door open.

"Oh. We had the door closed because we were changing, and had got our luggage together and were about to leave when the latch made a clicking sound, and the door opened up right in front of us. And there was no train going by."

Jean had to tell her about the haunted room, but he assured her the spirit was harmless and simply liked the door open. The nun has opened the door to the King Room on other occasions and has been even more active. [For our own ghost experience in the King Room, see the afterword.]

The Ghost in the Cemetery

This incident did not happen in L'Auberge Clémence itself, but behind the building in a small cemetery, which served the convent as well as parishioners of the nearby Catholic church. A number of Jean's relatives, including his father, are buried there. "A lot of people are interested in the graveyard," Jean said. This was certainly true of two guests, a brother and sister, who stayed at the bed and breakfast one late summer and asked many questions about the cemetery. Jean told them some of the history of the graveyard—that his father and uncles, as well as two aunts, who were nuns at the convent, were buried there. The guests were very interested and asked if they could visit the spot. He agreed and volunteered to go with them.

It was dusk when they arrived, but there was still plenty of light. As Jean escorted the two people around the gravesites, he noticed that they were not alone. Sitting on the ground reading a book at one end of the cemetery near two trees was a girl. She had on a white top and green shorts and was wearing blue suede shoes. Beside her was an old-fashioned green bike with blue balloon tires. Jean wondered why anyone would be reading a book in a cemetery as night was approaching. He recalled his experience:

We were walking by where the [Sisters of Our Lady of the Missions] plots are when they stopped, but I continued on because I wanted to go and find out who the girl was. I got to where I was only several feet from her. I couldn't see her face because she had her head down in the book. Just then the guest called me and asked me to come back because she wanted to know if this was my dad's gravesite. I went back and said yes it was, and then they wanted to see where my uncles were buried and we went through the whole graveyard. All along I kept my eye on this girl, and I was trying to see her face because she had her head buried in the book.

Jean took his guests back to L'Auberge Clémence, and then he returned to the cemetery. "But the bike was gone and she was gone." He was intrigued by who the girl might be. Elie has fewer than six hundred residents, and he was sure that even though he had not caught a glimpse of her face, he had never seen her before. He wondered who in town would know the identity of this person.

Later, Jean mentioned to Linda how unusual it was for a girl to be sitting in a graveyard reading a book at dusk. When Linda asked if he was seeing things, Jean replied, "No. Linda, I saw her. She was right there!"

The next morning, the young woman guest thought she had lost her wallet during their visit to the graveyard, so Jean accompanied her to search the grounds. Once they were in the cemetery, Jean said, "Oh, by the way, you remember when you called me, didn't you find it strange that that girl who was sitting there didn't even lift up her head to see that we were here?"

"What girl?" the guest asked.

It would have been impossible for the two people not to see the young person; the cemetery was small and, like Jean, the brother and sister would have to have noticed her. Jean had seen an apparition so solid and lifelike that he had mistaken her for a living person. He later checked the memorial stones in the cemetery, and there were a number of young people buried there who could have been the ghost. Because he never saw her face, Jean could not be sure how old she was. Frustrated, he declared, "The next time I see her in the graveyard at night, I'm going straight there and talking to her."

Many weird phenomena have happened at L'Auberge Clémence since it opened in 2002. When the third floor of the bed and breakfast was a forty-bed dormitory, the female students had little privacy, and during her visits, the nun continues to insist that she is not denied entrance to one of the bedrooms. If a guest in the King Room happens to be awake, usually in the early hours of the morning, he or she may hear the click, click, click of the latch as the late sister again opens the locked door.

TWO HOTEL HAUNTS

The Heritage Inn chain of eight hotels caters to travellers in Alberta, British Columbia, and Saskatchewan. The rooms are generally affordable, clean, and comfortable. However, two of the hotels have their own ghosts.

Charlie the Ghost of the Taber Heritage Inn

Taber is a small, southern Alberta town at the junction of Highways 3 and 36. Among students of the paranormal, the sprawling roadside community's one claim to fame is the entity known as "Charlie." The ghost is said to haunt the seventy-four-room Taber Heritage Inn Hotel and Convention Centre. While

Charlie has been mentioned on a number of Internet websites, details of the haunting are limited.

Although Charlie may be as many as three individual ghosts, the consistency of his behaviour suggests there is only one very active entity at the inn. He is a benign spirit who likes to make his presence known and enjoys playing practical jokes on the hotel employees. There is, though, something else—something difficult to describe—that seems to pervade one room of the hotel.

The eerie events at the inn may have occurred for more than twenty years. According to one story, Charlie died in a fire at the hotel. Research has shown that in the early hours of the morning, on Friday, January 12, 1979, a fire began in the sauna on the first floor and spread to the lobby. Smoke coursed through the rooms, killing two guests. The male victims occupied rooms on the first and second floors of the two-storey hotel. The cause of the fire was reported to be the thermostat in the sauna, which had been turned up to 121 degrees Celsius; the extreme heat was thought to have ignited the cedar boards that covered the walls of the room. Immediately after the tragedy, the notion that the fire was caused by either a negligent act or malicious intent was discussed within the community.[26]

However, the person whose death seems to be most closely identified with the haunting of the Taber Heritage Inn may have had nothing to do with the fire. While the date is uncertain, probably sometime in the late 1980s, a guest died of a heart attack in room 125. The man's body was discovered in the bath. Evidence suggests that he is the most active entity in the hotel; Charlie does not act as if he were an angry spirit who died before his time, but as someone who, for whatever reason, has chosen to remain where he spent his last night.

A few years after the man's death, another guest stayed in

room 125. During the night, she was awakened by the sounds of someone splashing in the bathtub. She arose and checked the bathroom. Once she entered it, the sound stopped, and she noticed the bathtub was dry. A few minutes later she heard splashing again. By now the sounds were distressing, so she phoned the front desk and demanded another room. While the bathtub story cannot be confirmed directly, there is little doubt that it took place.[27]

Often the housekeeping employees feel uncomfortable when they are preparing room 209. Whether the room was associated with the fire death is unknown, but it is above the area where most of the 1979 fire damage took place. The only physical manifestation that something is wrong, according to one employee, is that every spring and fall a strange species of fly invades only that room. It is not surprising then that room 209 became known among hotel staff as the "possessed room." (Hotel personnel, incidentally, dismiss the idea that there is anything unusual about room 206—the location that many websites claim is the haunted room.)

Janet Wagner described an experience her co-worker, Sherry, a member of the housekeeping staff, had. Sherry was preparing a room upstairs. (The location of this room is not known.) As she left the room to obtain items from her service cart, she saw a figure in the hallway. Because he was standing so close to her cart, it was almost as though he was waiting for her to finish her chores so that he could return to his room. But Sherry noticed that although he was solid, he had a grey cast. She turned around toward the room to call Janet and when she looked back to the cart again, he was gone. In the few seconds it had taken Sherry to turn her head, the figure had vanished, but it was difficult for her to accept that the grey man was a ghost. She asked the housekeepers working at the opposite end of the hall if they had seen someone pass, but they had not.

A spirited incident at the Taber Heritage Inn's bar shocked witnesses.
COURTESY OF DIANE BELYK

At times, Charlie likes to "play" with the hotel personnel. Several years ago, Sherry and Janet were making up a room on the second floor when Sherry drew Janet's attention to something odd—the brass safety chain on the door was swinging back and forth. The window was closed, and the air circulation was not enough to account for the rapid movement of the chain, which continued to swing in a wide arc. The women, who were accustomed to the ghost's actions, simply told Charlie to go away. "He can be a playful fellow," Janet observed.[28]

Charlie's antics are not limited to the hotel rooms. In late December 2009, Shandel Brandics, a member of the bar and catering staff, was alone in the atrium completing the place settings for a banquet. Shandel was at the rear of the room when the quiet of the afternoon was broken by a clink, clink, clink sound coming from the tables at the opposite end of the room. It was as though someone was striking a spoon against a glass to gain attention. Shandel was so shocked she remained motionless.

Then, she recalled, "You could hear someone walking away. You could really hear [the footsteps] echoing."[29]

Several years earlier, an employee who was vacuuming at the rear of the atrium suddenly noticed movement in the linen skirting on one of the tables. The doors were closed and there was no breeze to account for the odd behaviour of the heavy material. Even more surprising, the movement of the skirting affected only one of the tables along the row. Among the housekeeping staff, this was simply another example of "Charlie's tricks."

Unlike most ghosts, who seem shy and perform only before a small audience of one or two people, Charlie has "played" before larger numbers. In 2007, one of the staff was serving behind the bar while four patrons sat on stools around the counter. She was busy preparing a patron's cheque while her customers were talking among themselves when suddenly, before the startled onlookers, one of the glass coffee cups hanging above her head flew through the air and smashed against the opposite side of the bar. No one was near the cup when it took flight, and there could be no rational explanation for the incident.

While Charlie seems to enjoy playing practical jokes, hotel employees do not always share his sense of humour. Some time ago, Janet Wagner was in the laundry room waiting for one of the industrial washing machines to finish. The washer was on the final rinse cycle when the door flew open and water gushed over the floor. As in all industrial washing machines, the door was fitted with a fail-safe mechanism to prevent it from opening when the machine was full of water. In this case, though, not only did the safety lock fail, but the regular latch also opened on its own. Furthermore, as Janet observed, it was particularly strange that the door had remained shut through all the cycles and opened only when she had returned to wait for the final rinse.

One day, when Janet and other hotel employees were in the coffee room during a break, the metal lid of a trash container seemed to pop into the air and then fall to the floor. The people could only look at each other in surprise.

Although no one has ever been able to describe the ghost, Charlie is not always completely invisible. According to Janet, "Sometimes you'd be sitting there and you feel like somebody is standing behind you. I can see out of the side of my eye something that looks black. But when I turn around there's nothing there." She is not alone. Janet said, "Others [housekeepers] have experienced the same thing."[30]

Another site frequented by Charlie is an area above the kitchen that is used as a changing room. Two bar staff at different times, and apparently unknown to each other, have reported hearing footsteps walking around the room when no employees should have been there. Other than through the kitchen, there is no access to this space, and no intruder has ever been seen entering or leaving.

Disembodied footsteps are not limited to the small room above the kitchen. About 2005, before the opening of the lounge area in the morning, employee Fenny Harpell was tidying the men's restroom when she distinctly heard footsteps. At that time no one should have been in the vicinity. "They sounded as if they were right outside the washroom door,"[31] Fenny recalled. She immediately opened the door to see who it was, but no one was there. Fenny does not know whether the ghost remains active there, for the lounge is no longer open in the morning.

While apparently no eerie happenings have taken place in the Tank 77 pub, an uncomfortable feeling pervades it late at night. Shandel Brandics often has the feeling she is being watched. "It's like someone is always looking over my shoulder," she said.[32] Other servers have had the same sensation.

Dave, the Ghost of the High River Heritage Inn

Although less than forty kilometres south of Calgary, the business centre of High River, Alberta, has the look and feel of a small town of generations past. It is a community where nostalgia reigns.

Farther out from the town centre are the big box stores, modern shopping centres, and hotels of contemporary Canada. Built in 1980, the seventy-five-room Heritage Inn Hotel and Convention Centre off Highway 2 was later renovated in 2005 and, while not ostentatious, it generally provides a pleasant, comfortable stopover. However, the High River Heritage Inn has a paranormal attraction not claimed by most hotels. In this case the identity of the ghost is almost certainly known. Dave is the name of the presence that haunts the High River inn.

Dave was the general manager of the hotel soon after it opened. The well-liked man died by his own hand in the suite that was his temporary home—room 203—but he has not left the hotel he managed. It seems that he had a favourite table in the café, and he occasionally objects when senior staff occupy it. According to Dave's successor, Rick Bart, "On a really busy day we come [into the café] early in the mornings, and we usually sit at table 12, and then the radio will go really loud in the kitchen and the pots and pans go all over the floor."[33] The lounge, too, seems to be a favourite area for the ghost. Servers have had the feeling that someone was standing behind them, but when they turn around, no one is there.

One of the scariest incidents happened in about 2008, to the then night manager, Tyrel McLelland.[34] About two o'clock in the morning, he left his office to go to the kitchen to get a cup of coffee. When he returned he could see a man sitting in his chair. He was solid, with dark hair, and was wearing a blue suit. Even more unnerving, his eyes were fixed on Tyrel.

The High River Heritage Inn is haunted by the ghost of a former manager.
COURTESY OF DIANE BELYK

While the apparition looked like a living person, no one should have been able to get to the office past the front desk. To enter his office doorway, Tyrel had to turn a corner, and in the short time it took him to do so, the figure disappeared. Even if the man had been able to move at incredible speed, there was no way out other than past the night manager. But of course that had not happened. The only explanation was that Tyrel had been staring straight into the eyes of the dead general manager. It was Tyrel's only encounter with the ghost, but it was frightening.

Dave died in room 203, and yet nothing unusual is ever reported in that suite. He appears to be interested in the operations area of the hotel, perhaps to make sure everything meets with his approval.

Although two hotels in the Heritage chain have their own ghosts, they bear different relationships to the hotels. In Taber, Charlie was certainly a guest; in High River, Dave was the general manager. Both entities are innocuous spirits who like to make their presence known to the staff members at the inns they haunt.

CHAPTER THREE
HAUNTED HOUSES

CAPTAIN HIGHLINER

When Thomas Henry Brown died in 1942, the final page was turned on a fascinating life. First-class seal hunter, master mariner, and, in his later years, successful businessman, Brown was for half a century a well-known figure on the streets of Victoria. As the years passed, the memory of the friendly, outgoing Brown faded, but he was not prepared to disappear into that eternal night.

In the mid- to late-1980s, Ken Bruce, his younger brother, and their mother, Dorothy, lived in a large blue house with white trim on Selkirk Avenue, not far from The Gorge—a narrow inlet that slices northwest from Victoria's Upper Harbour. The house had at one time been a large, upscale, single-family residence, but in 1959 it had been divided into two suites. The second floor could be reached only by an outside stairway at the rear of the house. The occupant of the upstairs suite was the owner, Gerry, who was a bachelor. He was a kind man who after work welcomed Ken's visits for tea. The older man was an expert horticulturalist whose work had taken him far beyond the confines of Vancouver Island, and his stories opened up a world yet unexplored by young Ken. The teenager also appreciated Gerry's counsel on the difficult decisions that came with approaching adulthood.

The ghost of "Captain Highliner" was seen in the
Selkirk Avenue home of Captain Thomas Brown.
COURTESY OF DIANE BELYK

Gerry's house was an old dwelling, dating to 1911, but it was
solidly built, with one wall extending to a little hill that sloped
down to the waterway. The neighbourhood was quiet and for
Ken and his brother, the large backyard gave plenty of room for
outdoor activities.

Although the house was comfortable, Ken couldn't shake the
feeling that there was something strange about it. He sometimes
heard footsteps on the partly closed-in porch, but when he
checked, no one would be there. On other occasions, the front
door would blow open, which was blamed on the wind.

As time passed, Ken's intuition seemed to be well founded.
One late winter afternoon, he and his brother were playing Atari
video games in the living room when they heard footsteps on
the long, narrow porch at the front of the house. Moments later
these were followed by the sounds of the front door opening
and closing, and then the shuffling of feet in the hall. Assuming

their mother had returned from work, the boys eagerly awaited her arrival, but to their surprise she did not appear. After some time, Ken recalled, "I got up and had a look, and there was absolutely nobody there."[1]

One afternoon, Ken's brother also witnessed a frightening episode while he was sitting in the kitchen, which was at one end of a long hallway leading to the front door. From his chair at the kitchen table, the boy could look down the hall to his bedroom doorway and then farther along on the same side of the corridor to the living room doors. Almost at the end of the hall was Ken's bedroom.

The boy was alone in the house, or so he thought. As he sat, he heard noises coming from Ken's room. Surprised, he looked up in time to see a dark silhouette emerging from his brother's room and crossing quickly into the living room. It had taken only a split second for the shape to move out of sight, but Ken's brother had no doubt that someone or something had been there. The only reasonable explanation was that Ken had returned home early, so he called out to Ken. But there was no answer. "I walked down the hallway, saying I knew he was there and to stop goofing around," he recalled.[2] He searched the living room but no one was there. He was moving down the hall toward Ken's room when the front door abruptly blew open. Frightened, the boy ran out the back door and up the stairs to Gerry's suite.

The basement was undoubtedly the scariest part of the house. The few small windows set high in the walls let in very little light, which gave the area a gloomy atmosphere. Because the only entrance was by the outside door at the bottom of the back stairs, the basement left one with the feeling of being closed in.

While the cellar ordinarily would have had little appeal for Ken, Gerry had a small workshop, which he allowed the brothers to use. At first, seventeen-year-old Ken's busy life made it difficult to find time for hobbies, but he had one project that he wanted to finish. In 1984, he was building a remote-controlled model boat, and The Gorge was a great place to launch it.

One evening in the late fall, Ken was working on his model in the workshop. As he concentrated on his project, the heavy wooden door opened with enough force to send it back against the wall stop. Ken paid little attention, assuming that earlier he had not closed it properly. Then, after a few seconds, the door shut on its own, making a loud creaking sound. After only a short time, it swung wide open on its hinges again. Still intent on his work, Ken did not bother to look up. Again, after a short time, the door swung back into its jamb.

The notion that something was wrong, though, had probably registered at the back of the boy's mind. The door was of rough construction with an old-fashioned lock. A gust of wind could have blown it open, but it was not a stormy evening.[3]

During the two earlier openings of the door, Ken had not stopped working. Now, for the third time, while he was reaching for a saw, the door swung wide open again, and Ken immediately turned toward it. The figure of a man that was facing Ken was clearly not of this world. He was large—nearly large enough to fill the entrance. The grey shape, silhouetted against a night like black velvet, seemed to be illuminated by an inner light. Although the outline of the apparition blurred into a ragged mist at the edges, his appearance was clearly defined. The ghost was an older man with the broad girth that often comes with middle age. He wore the traditional peaked cap and cloth coat with the three sleeve rings of a captain in the merchant marine. Fleetingly, the figure reminded Ken of the man in the Captain Highliner seafood commercials that were frequently on television at the time.

Ken began to panic. There was only one way out of the

cellar, and a ghost currently blocked it. Without thinking of the consequences, Ken took several steps forward and threw the saw with all his strength at his unearthly visitor. Then he closed his eyes and quickly went out the door. He ran up the rear steps and into the suite, where he told his brother what had happened.

Ken, like most city residents, had little knowledge of Victoria's maritime history and no idea who the man in the uniform might be. Nor did he have any idea what "highliner" in the Captain Highliner commercial meant. Although it is an uncommon term, the word has been used from the middle of the nineteenth century to mean captains who netted the biggest catch. Other fishermen of the fleet held these men in high regard.

The next day Ken had tea with his landlord. While his visits with Gerry were common, this time Ken had a special reason for seeing the older man. As he related what had happened in the cellar, Gerry did not scoff. Instead he said, "I've been waiting and waiting for a story like that, but nothing ever happened to me."[4] Other people who had lived in the house earlier had seen the ghost of the sea captain. From a drawer, Gerry took a yellowing old photograph of a man with a handlebar moustache wearing the distinctive officer's uniform and asked Ken if he recognized the person. On the back was the date 1909. Ken was staring at a picture of the frightening figure in the doorway.

Ken never again felt comfortable in the basement workshop, and his model remained unfinished. For him, this encounter proved especially scary because of the way the figure had blocked his only exit.

For Dorothy, Ken's mother, the story seemed too incredible to be true. She felt that Ken had imagined the entire thing, and she tried to lessen his fears by making light of it. Ken gradually seemed to put the incident behind him, and it would probably have been forgotten had it not been for a snapshot taken in front of the house two years later. In the photo, Ken, his mother, and his brother are standing in the driveway in front of the house. Behind Ken and to his right is the porch that fronts the three bay windows of the living room. The photo was unremarkable, and Dorothy filed it away with her other memorabilia.

Her sons had grown up and had lives of their own when she was looking through her pictures again. When she found the photo taken outside the Selkirk Avenue house, she noticed something she had not seen before. In the right bay window— the window nearest Ken—was the image of a man peering out at the camera. In the dark, recessed porch, the face was difficult to see, but under a magnifying glass, the features were discernible. The face was large, larger than that of a living person.

Very few genuine photos capture the images of ghosts as they appear on this plane. That is not surprising, because solid, lifelike apparitions are so rare. Like most images of paranormal origin, this one is not properly formed—part of the forehead and cheek, particularly, are blurred—but regardless, there is little doubt that on that summer day in 1986, the camera snapped an image of a ghost.

It may be asked why Captain Brown chose to haunt the Selkirk Avenue house. The answer could be that ghosts are rarely known to haunt premises where they were happy, and the years Brown spent on Selkirk were a low point in his life. The sudden death of his younger brother, Harry, shortly before he moved in, the absence of his adult son who was now pursuing his own life, and Brown's less exciting job as a coastal mariner after his years as a sealer could have weighed heavily on him. The ghost was not the young Tom Brown in his first years as a seal hunter, but that of the master mariner in his last years.

A photo taken in front of the Selkirk Avenue house about 1986
revealed more than Ken Bruce and his family. In the lower right front
window is the image of a man believed to be Captain Thomas Brown.
COURTESY OF KEN BRUCE

Another reason for the Selkirk haunting may have been the house itself. It has long been known that changes to a structure often produce paranormal activity, and in 1959, the interior of the house was changed drastically. The wide staircase leading to the second floor was ripped out, and the building was divided into two suites. Typically, paranormal occurrences resulting from reconstruction lessen over time. It seems that when Ken and his family moved in, the house had been quiet for some years.

Why did Captain Brown reveal himself to Ken and his brother? The best answer is that the boys reminded the ghost of himself and his brother. The brothers were relatively close in age—the Bruce boys were about four years apart, and six years separated Thomas and Harry. Ken, who was mechanically inclined, probably acted as teacher and role model to his brother, in the same way Thomas could have acted toward Harry one hundred years earlier.

Again, it is not difficult to conclude why the ghost of Captain Brown was attracted to Ken when he was building his model boat. Throughout much of Brown's life, the sea and vessels were close to his heart. However, it is hard to understand why he materialized in the cellar doorway. By blocking the exit, was he attempting to hold Ken long enough to give him a message, and if so, what could it have been?

Ken described the ghost as resembling Captain Highliner, which was ironic because among Victoria's sealers in the last years of the nineteenth century, Thomas Brown held an honoured place. The Victoria *Daily Colonist* reported in 1932, "Captain T.H. Brown . . . was at one time master of sealing schooners as well as a hunter of considerable repute, being in the class of 'highliners,' men who got the most sealskins during a season."[5] Thus it was that on that dark night in the fall of 1984, young Ken Bruce found himself frighteningly face to face with a genuine Captain Highliner.

DARK MATTER

When Bruce Pinard was nine years old, he and his mother, father, and two older sisters moved into a house in Victoria. Little did the family know that the dwelling held a dark force that had at times seemed almost tangible. The residence then had green wood siding and was one of two almost-identical houses on a rocky outcrop overlooking Oak Bay Avenue. How old the house was Bruce never knew, but he once found a newspaper dating back to 1912 stuffed in a radiator duct. The plain appearance of the house suggests that it was built for a family of moderate means, who were more concerned with maintaining their personal comfort than following contemporary architectural fashions.

There had been rumours in the neighbourhood of violence that might have happened on the property, possibly even before the building of the house. Two brothers, it was said, had been in love with the same young woman. A quarrel arose, with the result that one murdered the other. While this may explain why the house was haunted, the validity of the tale remains questionable.

Bruce had not been in the house long before he became aware that something strange was going on in it. He had been given the first bedroom at the top of the stairs, and like most children, he liked to sleep with his door open. Outside his room, the stairway led down to a landing, from which twelve steps carried on down to the main floor. In bed with the covers pulled around him, the boy lay awake for an event that occurred as regularly as clockwork. At a certain time of night—Bruce believes it to have been eleven o'clock—he would hear a faint creaking sound at the bottom of the stairs. It would be followed by a second creak, slightly louder than the first. Then a third, fourth, fifth, and so on, each progressively louder until the disturbing sound reached the landing below his bedroom.

The paranormal activity that took place in this Victoria home ranged from the bizarre to the terrifying.
COURTESY OF DIANE BELYK

By then, the ghostly tread seemed so loud as to be jarring. Then the event would be reversed, the sounds diminishing with each creak down the stairs. Bruce never heard the tromp of boots or shoes—it was as though someone wearing slippers were slowly making his or her way upstairs as far as the landing and then deciding to return down the stairs. The nightly happenings were terrifying for a child lying alone in his bed, yet he could not sleep until the unseen presence had completed its ritual.

The ghostly creaking on the stairs seemed to be a residual haunting, but not all events in the house could be so easily classified. Bruce's mother, Norma Pinard, once heard what sounded like two children giggling at the top of the stairs. Believing that it must be her young son, she went to his room, only to find him fast asleep. Shadows would also be seen on the hallway wall near Bruce's room, and no trick of light seemed to account for the forms.

Bruce also recalls lying in bed and hearing what he believed to be the voices of a man and a woman. Although he was never able to understand what was being said, the exchange sounded sharp, as though they were angry but wished to keep the matter to themselves. Puzzled, he would get up and look out his window at the neighbouring house to see if the voices were coming from there. Only three metres separated the two dwellings, but the angry voices seemed to originate not from next door, but from inside his room.

Over the years, the family noticed that when they were in the living room, the cats would react to something at the head of the stairs. As Bruce recalls, "You'd be sitting there watching television, and all of a sudden they would act really strange and their bodies would contort, and they would seem to be in slow motion looking up the stairway. And they couldn't take their eyes off what was up there, but there was nobody up there." It was not the typical behaviour of felines that were about to chase their prey. "It was like something they had never experienced before, and they were reacting like that." The cats would be unaware of what was occurring in the living room and completely absorbed by what no human could see.

Bruce's father, Bert, who was in the navy and whose duties took him away from home for months at a time, never liked to linger in the second-floor bathroom (which, as in many old houses, was across the hall from the toilet). Often when he was in the bathroom, he could not shake the feeling that someone was in there with him. At times the sensation was so strong that the hair on the back of his neck would stand up.

While it is common for children to have nightmares, they are usually soon forgotten. For Bruce, though, one has remained with him into adulthood. In his dream he was downstairs in the living room when the outside door handle turned and the door burst open. In the entrance was a figure dressed in a long cape. In the shadows, Bruce could see the face had a neatly trimmed beard. The dark eyes seemed to penetrate him. "When I dreamed about it, it was like its energy was crawling all over my skin. I could feel its evilness." Rather than facing it, Bruce forced himself to wake up.

Whatever the nature of the entity, it was certainly malevolent, for one night Bruce's mother awoke with the overwhelming feeling that she was being held from her shoulders to her knees under a vise-like pressure. As she slept, her arms had rested across her chest. Now that Norma was awake, her trunk and lower limbs, with her arms across her body, remained in such a grip that she was unable to free herself. She knew that the force was physical, for she could feel a stream of air tousle her hair. The apparent source of this energy was not far away: in the darkened room she could make out an old woman standing at the foot of her bed. How she looked and how long she remained visible are not clear, but the incident terrified Norma.

Another time, Bruce's second sister, Diane, was sharing the bedroom with her mother. Also spending the night in the room was the family cat. In the early hours of the morning, Norma was awakened by the half-meow, half-whimpering sounds cats sometimes make when they urgently want to attract someone's attention. Expecting to find their pet by the closed door, eager to be let out, Bruce's mother sat up in bed, but the hump below the bedspread revealed that the cat was sleeping under the covers.

As Norma turned in the direction of her daughter, who was in the other bed, she saw something that made her blood run cold. Hovering over Diane's upper body was a heavy mist. It took her a second or two to realize what was happening, for as she watched, the mist that covered Diane's face was entering her nose and mouth. Raising her voice, Norma called Diane's name, but there was no response. She quickly made her way to the bed and began shaking her daughter. Finally the girl opened her eyes, but she couldn't speak until she had a glass of water. Although she could recall nothing that had happened, she felt parched, as if she had been stranded in a desert.

The two frightening events his mother endured occurred before Bruce reached his teens. By the time he was thirteen, his oldest sister had married and left home, and because her bedroom was available, Bruce moved down the hall. He never again had to face the horrors of that first bedroom.

When he was fifteen, Bruce and his friend Vern naively obtained a Ouija board and invited another friend, Nancy, over to the house. No one else was home, and the three sat around the board at the dining room table. Nancy, who apparently had psychic abilities and had earlier heard stories of Bruce's haunted house, was reluctant to participate. However, because Bruce and Vern did not want to give up an evening's "entertainment," they persuaded her to add her finger to the top of the planchette.

The three young people had just begun to use the board when they heard someone running along the rocky trail at the back of the house. The muffled sounds of anyone using the path could be heard in the kitchen, which was at the rear of the house, but these sounds were different: "They were desperate steps," Bruce recalled. What struck the listeners with foreboding was that the dining room was isolated from the trail; that room was in the middle of the house, separated from the kitchen by a lath-and-plaster wall. Moreover, it was dark outside and the trail would have been virtually impossible to follow at a run. "You can tell a lot [by the sound]," Bruce observed. "We all looked at each other and said, where's that coming from?" There was something very unnatural about it. Nancy got up from the table and refused to participate. No one objected.

But as the years passed, strange occurrences continued to plague the home. The fact that Bruce lived in a haunted house was never far from his mind, but he tried to adjust to it.

One evening when he was sixteen, he returned from his girlfriend's house to find that no one else had arrived home yet. Against what had been his practice, he took off his shoes. "If something weird happened while I was alone and upstairs," he reasoned, "there was one window that was low enough to the ground that I could jump out."[6] His shoes seemed to offer some insurance that he would not injure himself, but he thought that he was no longer a child, and he would not allow the entity or entities to run his life.

Thus, for the first time he left his shoes by the front door, and in his stocking feet climbed upstairs and walked down the hall to the bathroom. He turned the water on in the sink, and suddenly he was aware of a noise coming from his mother's bedroom. He turned off the water and listened. The bed had an old spring mattress that constantly protested whenever anyone moved on it. The noise was unmistakable: "Somebody or something was on my mother's bed." Bruce heard a rhythmic squeak, squeak, squeak repeated over and over. When he had walked down the hall earlier, the door to the bedroom had been open and no one could be seen. He closed and locked the bathroom door and yelled, "Who's there?"

The only reply was the continuing, rhythmic squeak, squeak, squeak that was so frightening.

Finally, in desperation he called out, "I've got a knife in here!"

There was no interruption in the noise that continued for fifteen minutes. Finally it stopped, and was followed by louder protests, as if the weight of two bodies had stood up from the bed, releasing the pressure on the springs.

Then the house fell silent. "I stayed in the bathroom for I don't know how long before I got the nerve to open the door and run like hell down the stairs, across the living room, out the door, and outside because I felt safe there. I was just praying for somebody to come home."

Over the years, one of the weirdest features of the house left witnesses shaking their heads. The master bedroom faced the front of the house, which, at night, was brightly illuminated by the streetlights of busy Oak Bay Avenue. With the drapes open, the light cast a peculiar image upon the head of the bed. It was a dinner party in progress, with the participants as distinct as in a photo negative. It was so clear Bruce declared:

> You could see a woman who had her hair that flipped up on the ends. She was wearing an Empire gown—you could see the cut, you could see the straps, you could see the tone of her skin was different in the shades of light and dark. You could see a man in the background with a suit on. You could see all kinds of things going on.

The image was clearest when the family first moved into the house, but over the years, it began to fade. Obviously there would have been no dinner party in the master bedroom, but most of the paranormal activity took place on the second floor where the room was located.

After the Pinard family moved away, the house was turned into suites, and Bruce was always curious as to whether the people who lived there were experiencing the haunting. Finally one day, he approached a tenant and asked if he was aware of anything unusual about the house. No—the man had not observed anything strange. The division of the house into suites seems to have excised the dark matter that had for so long been active in the dwelling.

This home in Fernwood, in Victoria, is the oldest house in the area and had so many owners during its long history that discovering who haunts it is impossible.
COURTESY OF DIANE BELYK

THE OLD BELL PLACE

Given the many people who have lived and probably died within this old building, it is impossible to say who haunts the brown-shingled house in the Fernwood neighbourhood of Victoria. Unlike the grand houses that still survive in some areas of the city, the Fernwood house was not built with the idea of style in mind. It stood on several acres in one of the oldest areas of the city, and when the house was erected, it would surely have been described as a farmhouse.

Although the house is dated in Victoria city records to about the turn of the twentieth century, it seems likely that some sort of crude cabin may have predated it, and that this older structure could even have been incorporated within the new house. During the early years of the twentieth century, the building also served as a boarding house for working people, many of whom were employed at the British Columbia Electric Railway car sheds, the neighbouring gas plant, and an iron works.

During the First World War, as many of the young men left for the front, the house could not be rented and was unoccupied for months at a time. In 1920, it became the residence of an orchardist, Thomas R. Bell, who established fruit trees on the land and sold the harvest in the city market. Bell remained in the house for some time, but the wet coastal weather often ruined some of the fruit crop, and eventually he sold the house to work as a gardener elsewhere. The addition of Bell's garden, with its rare roses and beautiful fruit trees, seemed to firmly tie the orchardist to the house and property.[7]

As Victoria's population grew, there was pressure to subdivide the acreage and even decrease the size of the lot where the large house stood. The result was that the house itself underwent drastic changes.

When Drew and Marie Fidoe bought the old Bell house in

July 1989, they were interested in preserving Victoria's old homes and, while it was not in the same class as some of the city's large Edwardian manors, it had a certain charm that appealed to the couple. Although the lot was comparatively small, mature cherry trees cloaked the grounds at the side of the house.

The house itself retained few of its original fixtures. In the kitchen was an old gas stove with a very long, narrow oven that puzzled Marie because it seemed unsuitable for preparing family dinners. (In the early 1930s, a baker who had a business nearby owned the house, and the stove was ideal for baking the goods he could take every morning to sell at his shop.) Drew and Marie looked forward to restoring the house to how it looked more than eighty years earlier, but little did they realize the difficulty of the task they had taken on. Furthermore, it was soon apparent that at least one of the old home's former occupants had remained behind to oversee the changes to his or her residence.

Not long after the moving van arrived with their furniture, the Fidoes realized that there was something eerie about their new home. The hallway opposite the closet at the top of the stairs was one spot where, as Drew recalled, "You always felt cold—whether it was hot out or cold out. There was always a chill there."[8] The couple tried to place the cage with their two cockatiels there, but the birds became so upset their owners had to move them.

Also, the second bedroom on the upper floor was unusually cold. "Some people would think old house, no insulation, but it was a different feeling," said Drew's mother, Lynda Gold. During the time Drew and Marie lived there, the room was not used as sleeping quarters. Instead, a small room on the main floor served as a second bedroom.

As is common in houses of that age, it was impossible to climb the stairs leading to the second-floor bedrooms without being heard. After they moved in, Drew, who was in the navy, was often away at sea. Marie had thought noisy stairs would give her a feeling of security, for "no one could sneak up on you in the house."[9]

It soon became apparent, though, that the distinctive pattern of progressive creaks up the stairs did not have to be triggered by the weight of a living person. Marie recalled that when sitting alone in the living room, she would hear the noises on the stairs. "I wouldn't hear the footfalls . . . only the creaks and it would be in the right pattern. Startled, I would say, 'Drew is that you?' And I'd turn around and there would be no one there." On some occasions the creaking stairs were particularly frightening because the pattern would be heard over and over again.

The couple had not lived there long when Drew was away at sea and Lynda came over from the mainland to stay with her daughter-in-law. While Marie had retired to the couple's room on the second floor, Lynda had gone to bed in the small room on the main floor. Some time later she was awakened by Marie's voice, calling to her to come upstairs. When Lynda climbed the stairs, Marie said, "I think I can hear something in the house." Lynda jumped into bed beside Marie, pulled the covers up, and listened. "And then we heard *somebody* walking up the stairs."[10] The sounds were an increasingly louder pattern of creaks, just as if someone were on the way to the second floor. When Lynda checked the staircase, there was no living person in sight. It was the first time that Marie and Lynda were absolutely sure the house was haunted.

When weight was applied to the last step before the upper landing, it creaked loudly, loudly enough for the noise to penetrate Drew and Marie's bedroom, even when the door was closed. At first the couple was alarmed, because they thought they had intruders, but the noise happened so frequently that they soon accepted it as commonplace.

Unexplained sounds were not limited to the stairs. Above the kitchen at the rear of the house was an attic used for storage. Without enough height at the peak to allow the average man to stand up, the area had remained unfinished, but it provided enough room for someone to walk back and forth. When she was in her kitchen, Marie recollected, "I could hear footsteps up there, like somebody walking. It wasn't a mouse, it wasn't a rat, it wasn't a raccoon—it sounded like somebody walking."

For Marie, the most frightening incident happened one afternoon in the bathroom. The house had been built without toilet facilities, but sometime later a bathroom had been added under the main floor stairs and extended to take space from an adjoining room. It had not been modernized and retained its claw-foot tub and a toilet with a raised, wall-mounted tank.

On this occasion, Marie was tidying the bathroom. She was alone in the house and working at the sink. To her right, about two metres away, was the toilet and a cleaning brush in a plastic holder. As she was standing at the basin, to her amazement the toilet brush, "came flying out of the corner [flipped] end over end, and landed at my feet." Marie postponed further bathroom tidying.

Later, when Drew arrived home, they decided to confront the entity that had frightened Marie. She said, "I don't know who you are, and if you want to live here that's fine. But throwing stuff—you're scaring me and I don't like it. Please don't do that again." Whoever or whatever was haunting the Bell place must have been listening, for this event was never repeated.

As the Fidoes worked on the restoration, it soon became obvious that the task was far greater than they had anticipated, and in June 1991, the couple sold their house and moved a short distance away. One afternoon, Marie and her mother-in-law took a walk back to Fernwood, and when they passed Marie and Drew's former home, they happened to see one of the new owners in the front garden. They stopped and chatted with the woman, and she invited them in to see the work she and her husband had completed.

When they reached the second-floor bedroom, Lynda experienced the strange cold sensation that she remembered. Curious, she asked the woman, "Do you feel anything in this house?"

The owner replied, "Is this house haunted?"

"Well, we had things happen."

The woman said, "That's why my dogs won't go in this room."

TWO CHILDREN

"Everything that happened there seemed so playful," Jane Dawe recalled, although some of the occurrences left her shivering. In the late fall of 1995, she and her twelve-year-old daughter, Lyndsi, and Jane's roommate, Kevin, moved into a house on Vancouver Island. The house seemed to be well suited for them. The rent was not unreasonable, the place was bright and comfortable and close to Kevin's work, and Tanner Road in Saanich was a quiet, pleasant neighbourhood. At the time they had the 1970s-era white stucco house with the beige wood trim to themselves, because the owner had not yet completed the basement suite.

The first indication that something was odd about their new home was a stubborn refrigerator door that would not stay shut during the night. While it might have been possible to come up with explanations for this, other incidents were more difficult to explain. Some mornings the videocassette recorder (VCR) would be turned on, and at other times they awoke to the sound of the television set, which had been turned off the night before. Kevin worked the night shift, and only Jane and her daughter were usually home during these hours. But while these events were puzzling, Jane did not find them frightening.

The evenings were also times of unexplained occurrences. While Lyndsi and her mother were watching television in the living room, the light would suddenly decrease in brightness. Since they were the only two people in the room, it was clear that no one had touched the dimmer switch. The lights controlled by other dimmer switches throughout the house also fluctuated in this way. Although the switches could have been defective, it seemed unlikely that so many electronic devices could malfunction around the same time. It was these many small episodes that added up to something extremely unnatural about the house.

One event seemed to point clearly toward a supernatural explanation. Not long after they had moved in, Jane and her daughter were watching television. She had lit a candle to create a pleasant atmosphere on the dark winter evening. When it was Lyndsi's bedtime, Jane wet her fingers and snuffed out the candle before leaving to prepare Lyndsi's room for the night. When she returned, to her surprise, the candle was again burning brightly. Jane asked her daughter why she had relit it.

"Mom," Lyndsi said, "I cross my heart I didn't do it."[11]

Jane was now convinced that she, Lyndsi, and Kevin were not the only inhabitants of their home.

Another mystifying occurrence involved Jane's collection of watches. In her room there was a large ornate mirror with shelves, into which Jane had mounted cup hooks supporting twenty or so watches. Jane recalled, "There was one particular watch that would start to swing on the hook. I could stop it, make sure it was absolutely still, let go of it, and it would start to swing again." Jane switched the watch with others, but it continued to swing. She and Lyndsi, transfixed, would watch it swing on its own. The watch's bright blue face with yellow hands seemed to lift one's spirits, and it was the kind that would have also appealed to a child. The movement of the watch on the hook happened so often that it became something of a party trick—when friends came by they often asked to see the strange antics.

On occasion, Jane's friend Ruth Anne would stay overnight, sleeping on the sofa in the living room. On the opposite wall was a rocker-recliner chair that creaked loudly whenever someone moved in it. One night Ruth Anne slept over, and in the morning she asked who had been in the living room during the night. When she was told that no one was up, she explained that, in the darkness, she had heard the distinctive sound of creaking springs as the chair rocked back and forth. Jane usually tended to dismiss such happenings as a joke so as to not frighten her friends.

Eventually, the owner finished the basement suite, which he then rented to a female tenant. The woman kept to herself, but one day when Jane was returning from work, the tenant approached her. She mentioned the noises she heard upstairs during the night and wondered about the odd hours Jane, Lyndsi, and Kevin kept. To Jane, the query made no sense. What possible noise could there be? She worked during the daytime, her daughter attended school, and her roommate worked the night shift, but throughout the night, their downstairs neighbour claimed, she could hear footsteps. Again, Jane passed it off lightly as the ghost. However, the haunting was a serious matter.

Most of the activity took place in the living room, where Jane and her daughter spent many evenings. The impression that they were not alone was frequently strong. She would often feel a cold sensation pass along her body, as though something was going through her. "It was like a ray of sun passing over your body," Jane said, "but icy cold instead." The feeling was very unnerving.

In 1997 Jane took another job, and in order to clear out unnecessary goods, she and her daughter arranged a garage sale. One of the women living in the neighbourhood stopped by and asked if they knew the history of the house. Jane asked, "What do you mean?" Her neighbour went on to explain that there had been a murder-suicide in the house involving two children. As she related the details, everything began fitting into place. Most of the activity in the house seemed typical of children, and Jane concluded it was their ghosts haunting the house on Tanner Road. Later, she spoke to the owner of the house, who confirmed that indeed a tragedy had taken place there.

Eleven years before Jane, Lyndsi, and Kevin moved into the house, a middle-aged couple and their two children lived there. The boy, sixteen, and the girl, fourteen, had developmental disabilities and had been placed in special classes (the girl, though, had apparently dropped out of school at the time of the homicide). According to one neighbour, "They were a family who kept very much to themselves," but the parents were described as caring lovingly for their children.[12]

On the evening of October 22, 1984, the husband returned from work to find his wife and daughter dead in the garage. A hose had been attached to a vehicle's tailpipe and run though a side window. Police found the body of the son in one of the roughed-in rooms in the basement. He had died as a result of wounds to the head. The father was so distraught he could not identify his wife or children—that had to be left to a neighbour.

Not long after their garage sale, Jane and Lyndsi moved to Vancouver, where Jane began a new job. However, they soon discovered that they had not escaped the playful ghosts of Tanner Road. In the late fall of 1995, she and Lyndsi would wake up to find the VCR turned on or the television playing. Their earlier experiences had convinced Jane that there was nothing malicious about the two children who haunted their dwelling.

The house on Tanner Road had frequently been the meeting place for Lyndsi's friends, who would spend hours on the trampoline in their large backyard. Jane, too, had friends who stopped by for coffee. Thus she concluded it wasn't surprising that the two presences attached themselves to the two people at the centre of what was a happy home. However, this was not where the ghosts belonged. One day Jane spoke to them directly, telling them that while they were welcome, this was not the place for them and that they really ought to move on. After those words, neither Jane nor Lyndsi ever experienced anything unusual in their new apartment. "It was almost kind of like they needed permission to be to free," Jane said.

The mark of the terrible incident was not quickly forgotten, and even today, after more than a generation, local people recall what happened on that October day. It can be hoped that these children have now found a warm and loving place.

A photograph of the front view of the Stave Falls
Powerhouse, taken sometime in the 1930s.
COURTESY OF THE MAPLE RIDGE MUSEUM AND ARCHIVES, PI866

CHAPTER FOUR

HAUNTED MUSEUMS

THE GHOSTS AT THE POWERHOUSE

Although British Columbia's Stave Falls Powerhouse produced its last kilowatt of electricity on March 22, 2000, the site continues to serve as an interpretive centre for the public. At the decommissioned facility, BC Hydro guides explain the operation of a generating station that was once the primary source of electrical power for Vancouver and the surrounding area. Yet after the last tour group has left for the day, the entire structure is charged with another kind of energy—a power that originates beyond this earthly realm.

In August 2004, not long after he began working as a guide at the powerhouse, Tim White had a meeting with one of the ghosts that haunt this huge building. Because he had been taking an evening course group on the tour, he had worked well beyond his usual hours. It was not until ten o'clock that the last student exited from the visitor centre. After Tim finished some paperwork and other routine tasks, it was at least another hour before he was ready to return home.

Because of a series of break-ins in the parking lot, Tim had parked his recently restored 1981 Ford F150 truck in the deck area in front of the building. The area was secured behind a fence with a metal gate. Since the fence was part of the building's elaborate intruder alarm system, he had to open the gate, drive his truck through the opening, lock the gate again, and return to the building to set the alarm system before he could leave.

When Tim reached his vehicle and turned the key in the ignition, he heard only a click, click, click sound from under the hood. The engine would not turn over. He would have thought that his battery was dead if it had not been that the headlights had come on. Tim tried again, but there was only the same clicking sound. Thinking he would have to phone his father at that late hour for help, he happened to glance back at the power station. There, clearly visible in the third window from the entrance, was a man. Every second bank of lights in the gift shop was routinely left on, so Tim had a clear view of the intruder.

He was clean-shaven, with a sharp jawline and hair that was somewhat dishevelled. From where Tim was, he could see only the figure's upper torso. The shoulders of the dark suit the man wore were clearly defined in the lighted room. "My first thought was my gosh, I didn't lock the doors. This isn't good."[1] Tim turned his attention back to the truck, but again the engine failed to start. When he looked up at the window again, the figure had vanished. Tim turned the key once more, and now the engine started immediately. The entire incident had lasted a few seconds—long enough for Tim to count which window the figure was looking out of and to get an accurate view of the man's appearance. It was as if the trespasser were boldly challenging Tim to do something about the intruder's presence in the building.

Tim was sure that the late-night visitor was a burglar who was in the powerhouse. When Tim reached the entrance doors, he found them locked. It was of course remotely possible that a thief had concealed himself until everyone had left, but this was unlikely, for visitors were counted in and out. "It's not my job to apprehend this guy," Tim said.[2]

In 1980, the inlet valve for unit 5 was the site of a fatal accident.
COURTESY OF DIANE BELYK

What the intruder would not have known was that an extremely sophisticated alarm system protected all areas of the building. All Tim had to do was arm it and wait for the man to trip a sensor sending an alert to police—it would take only a matter of minutes. Tim set the alarm and waited—nothing happened. The panel displayed the "active" light, and it would have been impossible for anyone to move more than a few feet in the building without triggering one of the sensors. Perplexed, Tim finally drove home.

As is common, only after the person has had time to reflect on the incongruity of an event do its paranormal aspects become clear. Beyond the obvious fact that the intruder failed to trigger the building's sensors, there are other puzzling questions. Given what happened later, Tim's inability to start the truck goes beyond the bounds of mere coincidence. It is also entirely illogical that a thief would have shown himself in the window and stared audaciously down at Tim. Further, the fact that a burglar would have set out on his illegal activities wearing a suit seems odd, at the least.

For Tim, who had until then not believed in ghosts, the episode was his first experience with the paranormal. Later he would have many more encounters with the ghosts that haunt the powerhouse.

Who are the entities at the power station? Ghostly phenomena, according to paranormal theory, are usually the result of tragic deaths. During the first years of the twentieth century, fatalities occurred during the construction of the dam and powerhouse. Stave Lake and the dam spillway were the scenes of many drownings, which may account for some of the ghosts that haunt the facility. One drowning took place within the powerhouse itself.

None of the electrical generating units have been replaced since the station was built. The last generator, unit 5, was added in 1925 when the dam was raised, and it was the most unreliable. In the early spring of 1980, powerhouse operators noted a significant drop in power output from unit 5. Believing that something was wrong within the penstock (the large tube that transports water from the lake), electrical power and water intake were shut down.

On Friday, March 7, 1980, a twenty-seven-year-old industrial scuba diver was called in to inspect unit 5.[3] What no one had realized at the time was that a leak inside the penstock would prove to be fatal—the water through the turbine inlet valve was moving more swiftly than anyone imagined. Plant supervisor Sandy Gillies and sub-foreman Jim Hinds accompanied the young man to unit 5. As Jim Hinds recalled, "Just before he climbed [down the ladder into] the unit, the plant supervisor said to me, 'How would you like to do that job?' I said, 'No, you couldn't pay me enough to do it.' The diver looked up and said, 'A piece of cake.'"[4]

When the man released his grip from the ladder, the water sucked him down the penstock. The wetsuit he was wearing acted like a poorly fitting drain stopper, partially sealing off the tube, and forcing the pressure to build up behind his torso. The result was that blood rushed from the diver's brain to the lower regions of his body. The unfortunate man was unconscious within seconds, which caused the mouthpiece carrying his oxygen to slip away.

Within a short time, by forcing water into the unit to equalize the pressure, the powerhouse personnel were able to recover the diver, but it was too late. Years later, an employee at the visitor centre would be, in a bizarre way, reminded of the accident.

One of the greatest difficulties workers faced in the massive generator hall was the tremendous noise produced by the five units. Since the station operated continually, employees were unable to distinguish the most common form of ghostly phenomena: sound. The uncomfortable working conditions—the units also generated considerable heat—and the need to keep a close eye on the machinery to ensure personal safety would have made it difficult to notice much else in the working environment. Yet unexplained occurrences did take place.

In the early 1970s Dennis Roberge was a part-time floor man working the night shift at the powerhouse. Only two people were on duty during this time: Dennis and the operator who monitored the electrical output and water levels behind the dam. Dennis's duties included completing a tour of the generator hall every hour to ensure that the machinery was running properly.

During one shift, when Dennis was finishing his rounds, he noticed that a door leading to a storage room was open. Believing someone had forgotten to secure it, he closed and latched it, and then continued on. On his next tour he was surprised to find that the same door was open. The only conclusion Dennis could reach was that the operator was playing a joke on him and had slipped down the stairs to open the door.

On his next tour Dennis varied his routine by making sure the operator was not out of his sight before he entered the hallway where the storage rooms were. But to his amazement, the latch had been lifted and the door to the room was open again. It was always the same door. And on later tours, he repeatedly found it open. In the logbook he was required to fill out after each tour, he noted that a "ghost" had been active in the generator hall. Later, other graveyard shift floor men noted the same ghost.

Only after the powerhouse ceased operation and the visitor centre opened was the full extent of the haunting realized. For the visitor centre coordinator, Janis Shultz, the facility has been the scene of many strange happenings.

The opening of the storage room door has continued for more than thirty years. When the station closed and the facility was repurposed, the employees found that the same door leading off the history hall also acted oddly. Although it should have been closed, it was repeatedly found open. Tim, who often did final rounds in the evening to make sure everything was secure, would be blamed when the door was found ajar in the morning. Finally, in desperation, he placed a screw in the jamb to prevent it from moving. While Janis did not know the story of the door that would not remain closed, she and Tim had long been aware that that storage area had been known as the "Ghost Room."

It is probable that many of the ghosts that haunt the powerhouse at Stave Falls are voyageurs, that is, those who have died in or near the area and have migrated to the powerhouse. The strong energy field associated with the power station may act as a magnet for such phantoms.[5] It is certain that many of them are strong presences and can freely move into the atrium, which was added after 2000.

At the beginning of the tours, a short video about power generation is shown in the theatre. As Tim was leading a group, one of the visitors in front of him stopped without warning, so abruptly that Tim almost ran into her. She said to him, "There's bad spirits here. I have to leave." Despite an offer of a ticket refund, she did not wait but walked hurriedly out of the building.

The haunting of the powerhouse was not common knowledge at the time, and she was right that ghosts reside in the facility. There is no evidence that they are really malevolent, for they have not hurt anyone, yet it is certainly true that at least one presence, the man in the window, seemed to enjoy terrifying Tim that night.

Other apparitions have been a part of the building's eerie history. Most common are reports of "corner of the eye" sightings that are frequent in many hauntings, but other visual phenomena have been witnessed. Although during most of its operation the powerhouse employed only men, one of the presences at Stave Falls is a woman. One afternoon at closing time in 2006, Carrie, a tour guide, saw someone near unit 5. The apparition was solid and was mistaken for a living person. The guide could give a clear description of the woman, who was wearing a long, floral dress with her hair arranged in a bun. When Carrie told Tim, he said it was impossible, for all the customers had left. Carrie replied, "No, no, I even talked to the lady and she nodded and walked away."[6] A search of the building disclosed that no paying customer remained.

On the lower floor, shadow sightings also have occurred. Tim recalls two very clear events that can only be described as indirect expressions of apparitions. Probably the most frightening experience occurred when he was walking down one of the metal stairways leading to the generating hall. When he reached the landing, he stopped for a moment and noticed how the light streaming in from the large, north-facing windows was casting his shadow upon the floor below. Then he saw the dark outline of a human figure quickly move up behind him and then stop. Thinking that someone was wishing to pass, he turned around. No one was visible. The event left him shaken.

Tim had a similar experience on the lower floor at the bottom of the stairs near the direct current, or DC, room (which holds the equipment that once charged the electromagnets). He was sweeping the floor when he noticed a shadow figure on the wall. "It was like someone walked up behind me, throwing their shadow behind mine," he said. The dark shape had a human form and could be seen "clear as a whistle."

This location seems to be an active site. After work on a very hot day in August 2009, Tim, his wife, Serena, and her friend Jan came in to prepare the deck overlooking Hayward Lake for a special event. As they walked through the building, "it was so hot," Tim recalled, "the sweat was pouring off us." However, as they reached the area near the DC room where he had seen the shadow, Tim happened to look back to see Jan with "goose bumps raising on her arms."

"What's wrong?" he asked.

Jan said, "Feel my skin."

He touched her arm. "She was so cold," Tim said, "that it was like she just walked out of a freezer."[7] There were no air ducts in the vicinity to account for her reaction. As they passed beyond the area, Jan was again perspiring in the sweltering heat of midsummer.

Like all active hauntings, most paranormal phenomena at the powerhouse are auditory rather than visual. In fact, unexplained sounds are extremely common. Because these events happen more often when the visitor centre is closed and only the senior personnel remain in the building, it is usually Janis or Tim who hears them.

On some occasions the events occur in the early morning. Not far from Janis's office near the visitor entrance is an aluminum grate that makes a metallic sound whenever someone steps on it. Janis observed that sometimes early in the morning, when she is working alone in the building, she hears that noise coming from the grate. As she said with a shiver, "No one will be there."[8]

On April 5, 2011, Janis began her workday by entering the visitor centre in time to hear the shuffle of chairs in the theatre. She was the first person to arrive and had to turn off the alarm before she could let herself in. There certainly could not have been a living person in the theatre. These morning shuffling sounds happen so often that now Janis almost takes them for granted. Often when she arrives in the morning, she has the feeling she is being watched—that there is someone, or rather, something in the theatre.

The feeling of being watched does not occur only in the theatre. A window-washer's sensation that he was under someone's gaze as he went about his work once so unnerved him that he reported it to the staff. Before starting the job, he had had no idea that the building was haunted.

One time Janis was alone in the generator hall when she heard a door slam on the second floor, in the area of the public lavatories. Given the weird events at the powerhouse, the sound did not concern her much.

When he was alone in the building late one evening, Tim experienced a similar occurrence. This time, though, the sound was much closer, and considerably more frightening. Tim had stayed well past his usual time when suddenly he heard a loud noise coming from the women's restroom. "It was the door slamming over and over again." Scared but aware he had work to do before he could leave, Tim phoned his wife so she could give him support. "It was not like a draft making a little bang, but all the time I was on the phone with my wife it was a loud bang as if the door was repeatedly slamming shut. When she answered, I never told her what was wrong. She said, 'What's that noise?'" He then told her what was happening and asked her to stay on the other end of the line until he finished and could leave. Tim clearly felt threatened, for he was trespassing in the domain of the ghosts during their most active hours.

The incident was unnerving, but with the support of his wife he managed to complete his work. "I thought," he joked, "if I don't do my job, what's more frightening, the boss or the ghost? I thought, ah, I'll take my chances with the ghost."

Staff in the visitor centre often hear loud banging noises coming from the generator hall. "Early in the morning Janis and I will be drinking coffee. We'll be the only ones in the building, and it sounds like there's a guy in one of the units hammering away," Tim said. The noises happen often and always stop abruptly when people enter the generator hall. These sounds are the most common of all the paranormal phenomena that take place in the powerhouse and are usually heard every two or three days.

Disembodied voices are both common and chilling. The words are always indistinct, but clearly people are talking. Tim heard a voice one day when he climbed on top of the penstock for unit 5 to examine the linkage that controls the large butterfly valve, once used to regulate the intake of water to the turbine. "It sounded like someone was talking really low or whispering," he recalled. He decided not to remain there and quickly climbed down.

Another day, Janis and two tour guides were on the mezzanine floor overlooking the generator hall when they heard people talking below them. Knowing no visitors had arrived that early, Janis and her co-workers searched the bottom floor, but no one was there.

The fan gallery, which is a confined area below the generator hall, is no place to linger, but sometimes it cannot be avoided. Tim routinely has to check the water pumps that control the seepage in this dimly lit, cavernous space. Few other employees will descend the narrow stairs leading to a location that is, Tim observed, "absolutely terrifying." Beyond the pump area, a narrow space extends into total darkness. Tim has heard the hushed voices here too.

Probably the most horrifying episode happened on the day Tim was in the fan gallery, and he heard a voice call out his name. The voice stood out clearly from the muffled voices he had heard so often before. Tim's name had seemed to come from very close to him, but he hoped that someone might have been shouting it from the generator hall. Later, he found that had not been the case. In the dark, humid gallery, whoever had called his name was very near him.

Janis has heard her name called in the history gallery, a museum with exhibits of electrical appliances that span much of the twentieth century. The voice was distinct—the deep resonance was as if a man had spoken. Yet no one else was on the lower floor of the building at the time.

One of the many odd happenings is the barking of a dog that seems to come from the area near the gift shop. Over the years, Janis, Tim, and other employees have heard the dog. Although it is never seen, Tim describes it as sounding about the size of a Labrador. According to him, "rather than a sharp bark, it seems to give a kind of a yelp."[9]

Why would a dog haunt the facility? Interestingly, new research has revealed that in 1965, the drowning of two men,

Joseph Bernard Grace and Gordon Allen, who were fishing on Stave Lake, was blamed on Allen's Labrador dog, Rover. According to New Westminster detective Bert Grace, Joseph Grace's uncle, "We'll never know exactly what happened. But we feel the dog must have capsized the boat. He was big and frisky."[10] While the bodies of the two men were later recovered, the dog's was not. In the glacial waters of the lake, the canine would eventually have been swept toward the dam, perhaps leaving his ghost to find a home within the powerhouse.

Beyond the sights and sounds that define most hauntings, other events have taken place at Stave Falls. Not long after she was employed at the visitor centre, Janis had an unusual experience while she was leading a tour. "I was walking backwards—we always walk backwards when we do the tour—and I felt I backed into someone." Janis turned around expecting to find a visitor, but no one was there.

It is true also that the power station ghosts haunt the electrical circuits. The stereo system, which plays music appropriate to the early years of the twentieth century, does not always perform as expected. When he closes for the evening, Tim routinely turns off the unit, but in the morning when the first person arrives, he said, "The stereo is on full bore. The music is just pumping out. Yet I know I turned it off." This happens frequently.

Unlike fluorescent fixtures, in which faulty ballasts can cause the light to be intermittent, halogen lights are reliable. However, even these lights act oddly near the DC room where Tim saw a shadow approach. "I've seen the light bulbs turn off and then turn back on again. The electricians have checked them and there's nothing wrong with them," Tim remarked. And, as Janis said, "I'll tell Tim a particular light is not working, and then it works when he goes to check it."

In October 2010, another weird episode took place in the

women's washroom. Dan, one of the guides, was checking the lavatory at closing time when he was almost overwhelmed by perfume. The fragrance was so strong as to be noxious. Dan quickly beckoned Tim to sample the overpowering aroma. However, when the two men entered the room, they could smell nothing. In the short time in which Dan had gone to get Tim, the odour had disappeared.

In 2007, Tim remained late one night during a period when an American network was using the Stave Falls complex to tape an episode of the television series *Smallville*. Tired and concerned about his ability to stay awake while he drove home after a gruelling, sixteen-hour day, he phoned Serena to ask her to pick him up.

"We were walking out of the building," Tim recalled, "and she had my cellphone. Serena said, 'What's this?'" The date on the display read a day, month, and year, twenty-seven years earlier.

Although at first it meant nothing to Tim, he had heard stories of the tragic death of the scuba diver in the generator hall. He did not know for certain the year of the man's passing, but he felt sufficiently unsettled to check further. He discovered that not only the year, but also the month and day corresponded with those of the diver's death.

Like Tim, Janis did not believe in ghosts. "When I came here I never believed in anything like that. And then one time something happens, and then another. I think it took me a good year to understand that something was going on."[11]

With the exception of the dog, Rover, only the apparitions can give a clue to their identity. The woman in the long dress, whose clothing suggests the 1930s, may have come to the powerhouse after her first haunt at the townsite was demolished to make way for a park. Yet this is only supposition.

While the identity of the apparition that Tim saw in the window of the visitor centre is unknown, the man was not someone who died on the job, for employees never wore suits in the building. The heat in there was withering. That his hair was dishevelled suggests that he might have died as a result of some form of trauma. But beyond these observations the identity of the intruder remains a mystery. What can be fairly concluded, though, is that the sheer number of paranormal occurrences at the powerhouse at Stave Falls leaves no doubt that there is a plane of existence beyond human understanding.

GALT MUSEUM

The entities haunting the Galt Museum and Archives in Lethbridge, Alberta, could have come from an old Hollywood movie, but they were not created from the imagination of a scriptwriter. There has been a litany of inexplicable experiences at the museum; however, the identities of these ghostly visitors remain a matter of speculation. One terrible death more than eighty years ago, though, has become inextricably linked to the museum haunting. "George" is the entity who may have good reason to haunt the corridors and rooms of what was once an old hospital. It is not difficult to believe that the circumstances of his death could have created a very angry ghost.

The old red-brick building that is now part of the Galt Museum was once the 1910 Galt Hospital, which also contained the School of Nursing. In 1955, it closed as a primary care facility but remained in the community's health care system as a rehabilitation centre and finally, in 1966, as the Lethbridge Health Unit. Because the building was too big for the health unit, two floors were completely renovated to become the city's museum. Eventually, the health facility was moved, and in 1979, the entire old hospital became the Galt Museum. Two later additions became part of the museum complex (apparently, these wings remain ghost free).

Some of the lore associated with the Galt haunting dates to the first decades of the twentieth century. One story that has been passed down through the years is about a young boy with appendicitis who was admitted to the children's ward. The nurses told him that whenever he needed help, he should ring the call bell. Although the death rate from appendicitis was not high, it occasionally claimed a life, as it did in the case of this boy.

In the early hours of the morning after his death, the nurses on night duty were shocked to hear the bell in the boy's former room ring three times. No other patient had been admitted to the ward, and the bed remained unoccupied. When they told the nurses arriving on duty about the incident, their dayshift counterparts found it too incredible to believe.

It is not difficult to imagine how frightening it was for the nurses when, the next night, the bell rang again three times. They demanded that the cord to the call bell be disconnected so it could not ring.

The day shift staff who were continually administering to their patients were likely to regard the events on night shift as the result of overactive imaginations. The number of staff during the night was small, so few people witnessed the occurrences.

However, the nurses' account of the ringing bell was verified. At two o'clock, when the boy's burial was taking place, the day shift staff heard one of the call signals ringing in the nursing station. As they looked up, they saw that it was the one in the room formerly occupied by the young male patient— the bell that had been disconnected earlier. It rang once, twice, a third time, and then ceased. This never occurred again.

Ghosts from the past are present in Lethbridge's Galt Museum and Archives.
COURTESY OF DIANE BELYK

The most famous ghost claimed to haunt the museum's old hospital wing is George. In 1931, while being wheeled into the automatic elevator that was to take him to the operating room, sixty-one-year-old George Bailey met with a gruesome freak accident. The malfunctioning elevator first crushed him between the closing doors, and then dropped him down the shaft to the hospital's basement. George's injuries were critical and he died soon after he was recovered from the shaft. His wife later sued the hospital, but she received almost nothing in compensation for her loss. While one would expect a wrathful male presence to haunt the museum, George seems to be anything but angry.

Jeff Small, a museum volunteer, was cleaning his paintbrushes in the museum workshop, near where George was retrieved from the bottom of the elevator shaft. The radio was playing in the room when suddenly Jeff was struck by the feeling that he was no longer alone. Before he had time to turn his head and look around, he heard a male voice say, "Hello."

"It wasn't a question, like 'Hello, is anyone there?'" Jeff said. "It was a statement."[12] When he turned around, he found that he was alone. Although Jeff had felt a presence on earlier occasions, this was the only time George spoke to him.

Galt Museum educator Belinda Crowson also received a weird greeting, but on this occasion the source could be clearly identified. About 2006, she was working in the office that she shared with a co-worker. Although her computer was turned on, she was not using it at the time and was busy with a project on her desk. Breaking the quiet of her office came a metallic voice that said, "Hello."

Her officemate raised her head over the partition and asked, "Was that your computer?"

"Yes," exclaimed Belinda in surprise.

Again the computer offered the greeting.

As far as she was aware there was no reason for the computer to speak, nor did it ever do so again.

George seems to spend most of his time in the basement near the old elevator shaft. Over the years there have been accounts of mysterious blue lights in the area. Lights flickering on and off and shadowy shapes moving along the walls have been reported, while sudden columns of cold air have also occurred.

George is only one of the ghosts that haunt the old hospital wing. The second-floor offices, which were once the children's ward, are a very active area. "If the [intruder] alarms go off anywhere in the building," Belinda observed, "chances are it will be on the children's ward."[13] One of the first stories concerns a researcher who was working late one night alone in the museum. As he left the building and walked toward his car, he happened to look up to the second-floor windows. To his astonishment, he saw two children looking down at him and waving. Over the years, the names that have become attached to the little ghosts are "Sarah" and "Alexander." Sarah appears to be about six, while Alexander seems to be between ten and twelve. Around 2008, a family with two young children arrived for a tour of the museum. Both children were looking up toward the second-floor balcony and waving. Puzzled, their mother asked them what they were doing. They said they were waving at the boy and girl "who were dressed funny."[14]

Evelyn, a staff member who has her office in what was once the children's ward, usually wipes down her monitor before quitting for the evening. When she arrives the next morning, fingerprints have mysteriously appeared on her screen.

Also on the old children's ward, the ghosts seem to enjoy playing with the lights. One evening near Halloween several years ago, Belinda was taking a tour of young people through the ward. As she was leaving she switched off the overhead bank of lights. Before the group had passed through the door the lights came back on. Belinda turned the light off again. Moments later the room was flooded in light. A third time she flipped the switch, only to have the incident repeated. Finally Belinda turned to the tour group and said, "They want the lights on tonight. We're leaving."

The tour group had been picked up, the museum locked, and the fire and security alarm armed; Belinda walked to the parking lot with her co-worker, who said, "I wonder if the lights are still on in the children's ward." They looked up and the area was entirely dark. But as they watched, the light came on. Because it would have required physically turning a switch to the "on" position, it was unlikely that the light coming on was a simple electrical problem. It could only be another of the odd happenings at the Galt.

Several people, when they were alone on one floor of the building, have reported hearing children's voices, apparently coming from elsewhere. A partial explanation may be that although the building is brick, outside sounds pass easily through the exterior walls. Depending on the time, the voices could come from children playing nearby.

It is easy, also, to confuse the nature of a sound. Late one evening, Belinda took several friends through the museum. When they reached the old children's ward, one person asked, "What's that clicking?" It sounded as if children were playing with blocks or dominoes. The next day, Belinda was talking to Susan about the sound. Susan, whose office was elsewhere on the second floor, said, "It's not dominoes; it's a typewriter." Apparently Susan had heard the click, click sounds for some time and recognized them as an old-fashioned mechanical typewriter.

Another ghost has been said to be that of a nurse, and it would not be surprising that, if she exists at all, the nurse would be drawn to the old operating room on the second floor, to what was once a critical section of the hospital.[15] Psychics who have independently toured the museum have remarked that this room is the most active area of the building. Belinda, whose office is in the old operating room, sometimes has the overwhelming feeling that she is being watched. "It's at these times," she said, "you know it's time to go home."

One morning when Leslie, Belinda's new office mate, arrived at the museum, she heard noises coming from Belinda's cubicle. Assuming Belinda had arrived early that day, Leslie called out a greeting. When she received no reply, Leslie thought this was rather rude but continued on with her work. It is not difficult to imagine Leslie's surprise when Belinda came in a few minutes later. There had been no other living person in the office.

Although there may be a good reason for an angry ghost to haunt the old hospital, the spirits of the Galt appear to be benign. Indeed, Belinda Crowson hoped they would be a little more energetic. "I just wish they'd clean my office," she joked. "If you're going to be here, be useful."

THE MARR RESIDENCE

The Marr Residence, one of the first houses built in Saskatoon, Saskatchewan, has two ghosts. The best known of these is the phantom that most people call "Charles," a quiet and studious young man. The other is a nasty fellow who remains in the basement. It is not wise for women to linger long in this entity's domain, for he particularly dislikes the opposite sex.

There were no "spirits" in early Saskatoon. The first settlers were members of the Temperance Colonization Society. Methodist minister John Lake's vision of a colony free of alcohol coincided with the Canadian government's plan to establish agrarian settlements in the Northwest Territories. Lake enrolled more than three thousand people who were willing to sign a pledge to abstain from alcohol and would purchase property from his land company. In 1882, he chose the location of his townsite on the South Saskatchewan River at a place where the water was shallow enough to be forded by horses and wagons. That the colony was 260 kilometres north of the Canadian Pacific railhead at Moose Jaw, where liquor flowed freely, was probably one of the reasons that the Reverend Lake accepted the land grant of 313,000 acres (126,667 hectares).

Alexander "Sandy" Marr, who was among the first tradespeople to arrive, built his house in 1884 in the new townsite. A stonemason, Alexander knew his trade, for unlike many prairie homes of the period, the foundation was well constructed.[16] In contrast to the sod huts that were the homes of less fortunate pioneers, the Marr Residence, with its wood siding, mansard roof, and dormers to let in the light, was built to last. Indeed it is the oldest house in the city still standing on its original site.

A well-dressed apparition has shared the upper floor
and stairway of the Marr Residence with the living.
COURTESY OF DIANE BELYK

In April of 1885, with the outbreak of the Northwest
Rebellion, the Marr Residence was commandeered as a field
hospital for wounded Canadian troops, and the family moved
in with friends. With the surrender of the Cree leader, Big Bear,
on July 3, 1885, the rebellion was over and the army hospital
was decommissioned. Alexander, his wife, Margaret, and their
family returned home.

Four years later, Margaret died, leaving the widower with
seven children to care for. In 1892, Alexander sold the dwelling and moved with his family to Prince Albert, Saskatchewan.
After he sold it, the Marr Residence remained privately owned
for the next eighty-seven years.

The building was restored by the City of Saskatoon and
designated a heritage site in 1982. The first floor was opened
as a museum that depicted the Marr Residence as it was when
it was an army hospital. The second floor was leased at first to

the Saskatchewan Association of Architects, and later to the Saskatchewan Society for Education through Art (SSEA).

Not long after the SSEA moved into the offices, employee Laurie was aware that something about the house was eerie. She would be working in her office when suddenly a sheet of paper would fly off her desk and flutter to the floor. It was as if someone had walked quickly by, creating a brief current of air. Alone in her office, she would have liked to believe it was simply a draft, but often when it happened the storm windows were in place, and there were no air currents.

An event that was far more frightening happened one Saturday when she and her twelve-year-old daughter stopped by Laurie's office to pick up something that she had forgotten. They had entered the building, retrieved it, and were about halfway down the front stairs when they heard a noise above them. The sound came from Laurie's office, which they had left seconds earlier. It was as though a heavy object had slid across a horizontal surface, such as her desk, and then had fallen with a dull thud to the floor. Both Laurie and her daughter heard it. They returned upstairs and Laurie unlocked the door to her office, expecting to find something on the floor by her desk, but nothing was out of place.

On another Saturday, Laurie stopped by the office. She parked at the rear of the house and, as soon as she entered through the back door, she could hear her office radio blaring. The afternoon before, when she left for the day, the radio was not on. When she attempted to silence it, the switch was already in the "off" position. The only way she could stop the noise was to unplug it from the wall outlet. She took the radio home with her, plugged it in, turned it on, and it operated properly. There was little doubt that there was something unnatural about the radio when it was in her office.

Laurie discovered that the ghost was not restricted to the second floor. At one time, there had been problems with the computer network and it was necessary to call in a technician. At the end of the day, he and Laurie were leaving by way of the dining room and, as they reached the kitchen door, something seemed to hold them back. Then the temperature dropped dramatically, and the dining room became extremely cold. The two people looked behind them into the front parlour where a rocking chair stood by the fireplace. While Laurie saw nothing, the computer technician was sure that there was a shadowy figure sitting in the chair.

While the ghost did not usually bother Laurie during normal working hours, he seemed to resent weekend visits to his domain. One Saturday afternoon in the late 1990s, the executive was holding a board meeting in the second-floor boardroom that opened onto the stairs. The members sat on each side of a long table, while at its head was the president. From her position she had a clear view of the open door and the stairway beyond. During the meeting, she happened to look through the doorway to see a man climbing the stairs to the landing. When he reached the landing he turned and climbed the few steps leading to the front room. She later described him as clean-shaven and wearing a formal, three-quarter-length jacket. As he walked up the stairs he was removing his gloves. Although the apparition was solid, there was something about him that did not seem right. The president turned toward Laurie and asked if the building was haunted. Laurie had to agree.

This was not the only phenomenon that occurred during an SSEA board meeting. The meetings were always held on Saturdays and, like many similar meetings, they tended to drag on longer than was necessary. One particular meeting had continued from the early afternoon until almost five o'clock, so long that the odd member could no longer stifle a yawn. On the wall hung a piece of Aboriginal art, a wooden staff ornamented with feathers and beads. Suddenly, the relatively light piece of art lifted off the hooks that held it in place and struck the floor with great force. Not surprisingly, the meeting was called to a close.

About this time, Laurie was working in her office when a woman happened to stop by. She mentioned that she had psychic abilities and was struck by the impressions she was receiving from the house. Laurie gave her a tour of the first and second floors, as well as the basement. Because the person was unaware of the incidents that had occurred earlier at the building, what she recounted was amazing.

Later she repeated her impressions before several members of the SSEA and the board that operates the museum. According to the psychic, two ghosts haunt the Marr Residence. One invisible presence occupies the basement. The other, a far more dynamic phantom, Charles, is found on the second floor. Charles boarded at the Marr Residence many years ago. His work required him to keep records, and he was proud of his penmanship. He took great pride in his hands, and always wore gloves to protect them. She concluded that he lived alone, was a bookish individual, and did not socialize with others much.

The paranormal activities that take place on the second floor are perhaps not difficult to explain. The ghost believes that the area belongs to him, but he now accepts that others also share his space. Charles becomes angry, though, whenever anyone intrudes upstairs after normal working hours—most of Laurie's problems with him happened when she dropped by her office on a Saturday.

Research later revealed that a Charles Gathercole, a clerk in a Saskatoon general store, B.A. Archibald and Company, boarded at the house in 1908. He died in September of that year, at age thirty-three, and was buried in Woodlawn Cemetery. No headstone was erected, which suggests he had no next of kin in the city.[17]

Strangely, no other record of a Charles Gathercole that matches what is known about him has been found in any Canadian sources, including birth and immigration records. Other than the meagre information that has been uncovered in Saskatoon, the life of the phantom of the Marr Residence remains a mystery.

About 2005, the Marr Residence board arranged a Victorian Christmas event in which guests were encouraged to wear period clothes. Several dozen people arrived in costume, including board member Dianne Wilson, who brought the seven-year-old daughter of a friend.

At the end of the festivities, all the guests had left except Dianne, two other board members, and the little girl. Moments before they were ready to leave by the rear door, the child turned to Dianne and said, "You know, I saw a man on the stairs and he was wearing a tuxedo. I could see right through him and he turned around and looked back at me."[18] By then the Marr Residence had gained a reputation as a haunted house, and Dianne thought the child was simply imagining the person.

The next day she phoned the child's mother and asked if the girl had enjoyed the party. "Well," her mother said, "she seemed to have had a good time, except that she told us this strange story about a transparent man in a tuxedo on the stairs." He had obviously left a deep impression. Interestingly, the girl's description of the ghost's formal attire tallies with that of another witness, the president of the SSEA. Both adult and child appeared to be describing a morning coat, formal day wear that was above a clerk's class but in keeping with a man who probably regarded himself as better than his "backcountry" fellow clerks.

When another Christmas party took place and Dianne arrived to set up for the event, she was met by Linda, another board member. Linda appeared puzzled and asked if there were any plumbing pipes through the walls in the front hall. Dianne replied that she did not think so, for as far as she knew the plumbing was at the back of the house. Curious, she asked if there seemed to be a problem.

"Well," Linda said, "just as I opened the front door, I heard what sounded like a marble rolling across a hardwood floor upstairs." There was of course no one on the second floor at the time.

In the basement, the psychic felt the presence of a man who in life was an unpleasant, filthy individual who took a bath only when he happened to fall into the South Saskatchewan River. He had a cabin on the land before the Marr Residence was built. According to the psychic, the person was a misogynist who particularly hated women who challenged him in any way. His wife had lived in fear of his anger. Fortunately, the psychic said, he was not a strong entity and could do nothing more than play tricks on the women who were in the building.

Long before she met the psychic, Laurie felt uncomfortable whenever she visited the basement where the art association stored its files. If she had to spend more than a few minutes there, she had the sensation that someone was watching her.

Laurie recalled when Ryan, a summer intern, began his first day on the job. Laurie went down to the basement to bring up the three-ring binder that held the training manual and was surprised to find it missing from its usual place on the shelf. The basement made her uncomfortable, and she did not like to spend more time than necessary there. After a thorough search she could not locate the binder and returned to her office upstairs.

Ryan volunteered to search for it himself, so Laurie described the binder and where it should be. Ryan walked down to the basement and minutes later he returned. In his hand was the binder, which had been on the shelf where Laurie had said it should be. There was no doubt that when she had looked for it earlier it had not been there.

On another occasion, an auditor arrived to complete the yearly report. There were no difficulties until they went to the basement to list the videocassette recorder (VCR), which the SSEA used for classroom presentations. It was not on the shelf where it was usually stored, nor had it been signed out for use. They searched the basement and upstairs rooms, but the VCR had disappeared. A week after the audit, Laurie was in the basement and happened to glance up at where it was kept. On the shelf in its storage space was the VCR.

Dianne, too, senses the man in the basement. "When he's there I get a little chill up my spine," she said. His presence is far stronger in the centre than at either end of the area. One experience she particularly recalled:

> We don't usually take the public to the basement because the stairs are steep and narrow and it's not really public space. But one day I had a small group of schoolchildren here with their mothers—these were ten- and eleven-year-olds from the advanced program—and they wanted to see the [haunted] basement. There were about four or five girls with their mothers in the basement and I was telling them about the ghost. One girl suddenly stiffened and said, "He's here—I can feel him walking past my shoulder." And you could feel the edge of this cold air mass. It was a defined edge and it moved across the basement.[19]

Charles clearly regards the Marr Residence as his space but was willing to share it with Laurie as long as he had time to himself. He was probably pleased when, in 2007, the SSEA moved to new offices; now he does not regularly share the second floor with employees. While the entity in the basement is a nasty ghost, he has not been a strong presence.

One of the ghosts seen in this former funeral home, now the Rose and Crown Pub, was a woman wearing a grey dress, white gloves, and a pillbox hat.

CHAPTER FIVE

SPIRITS IN A GLASS

ROSE AND CROWN

In 1983, when Dennis Madden attended a service at the McInnis and Holloway Funeral Home on Fourth Street South West in Calgary, he had no idea that he would be working as a bartender in the same building some years later. And, to his surprise, not all the spirits he would encounter were poured from a bottle.

C.M. Shaver opened his funeral parlour in 1903, and in 1935, in partnership with another mortician, moved to the location on Fourth Street. Funeral directors McInnis and Holloway later owned the firm and used the site until 1985. The old funeral home was bought by a popular band, the Irish Rovers, and in 1986 it opened as Calgary's first English pub–style establishment. Although an additional wing for the kitchen was added, changes to the building, which dates from the early 1920s, were kept to a minimum. In 1996, Larry Davis purchased the Rose and Crown from the Rovers.

The emotional energy supplied by patrons enjoying the good times at the Rose and Crown may be the reason for the extensive paranormal activity at the site. Thus it could be that the living may share common ground with ghosts: for both, "happy hour" may reinvigorate the spirit.

Soon after the Rose and Crown opened its doors, there were whispers that the pub was haunted. That was not unreasonable, given that the building had been a mortuary. When Dennis Madden began working at the pub in 1992, he soon had the sense that something about the old building was weird. "I don't know if it's the people that lived here, or that are buried here or cremated here, but there are lots of spirits or ghosts," he observed.[1]

Although he would be sure all the lights were out before he left, as he drove past the pub he would see a bulb on in the attic. Years earlier, the attic had been used as an apartment for a caretaker, and it is now one of the many psychically active sections of the building.

Often when he was alone at the end of a shift, Dennis had the feeling that he was being watched. It was usually accompanied by a prickly sensation, and the hair on the nape of his neck would seem to stand on end. This perception was strongest on the third floor. It has been left much as it was during the time the building was a funeral home, and the original wallpaper is still in place. Here, Dennis often had the feeling that someone was standing behind him, almost breathing down his neck. He would turn around to discover that no one was there—at least no one he could see. He caught glimpses, though, of a figure in the hallway moving toward the main floor kitchen. When he turned in that direction, no one was visible.

The pub had an array of unusual sounds that were particularly noticeable when the building was closed, but Dennis, who until several years ago was the night manager, could not account for all of these noises. As he recalled during a 2006 interview, "There are certain noises that an old building makes. The furnace, ice machines, coolers, and things—if you hear them for the first time you don't know what they are. But I've been here so long I know what they all are."[2] Yet one night after closing, as he and head bartender Al Hunter were on the main floor completing their last jobs before leaving, they both heard a rapping sound coming from the hallway behind the bar wall.

The noise was distinctive—like someone knocking on a hard surface. Dennis first thought that it might be a patron in one of the lavatories behind the bar, but both rooms were empty. He continued to make a thorough search of the area, but there was nothing to be found. He then checked the outside doors to make sure that they had been properly dead bolted, and no one could have got out. Nothing was out of place.

He returned to the bar in time to hear the rapping noises again. "It wasn't a rhythmic kind of knock," he recalled. Instead, it was a staccato: rap, rap . . . rap, rap, rap. People find such asynchronous sounds unsettling.[3] He looked questioningly at Al and asked if he had any idea what that was. Al, who had worked at the Rose and Crown since not long after it opened, could only shake his head.

On occasion, long after closing time, Dennis heard noises apparently coming from the kitchen, like the crashing of pots and pans and cookie sheets falling to the floor. When it first happened he was sure there had been a break-in. "I had my cellphone with my finger on 911, and I walked back to the kitchen and the door was dead bolted," Dennis said. "I checked the refrigerators in case someone was hiding in them, but no one was there." He looked toward the area where the pots and pans were stored. Amazingly, "there was nothing out of place!"[4]

The kitchen, which is in the new wing, has been a hotbed of activity. Early in the morning when chef Jason Gieck arrived for work, aluminum measuring cups would fly off the shelves, as if someone flicked them with their fingers and sent them into the air. Obviously, with so much work before him, the flying cups were an annoyance. But Jason and his staff soon discovered that if they said good morning to the unseen presence, the utensils would remain in place. "But if we forgot to say good morning," Jason said, "things would start falling off until we said good morning."[5]

It is unusual that these entities are not limited to specific locations but seem to wander freely throughout the building. According to Jason, who is a long-time employee of the Rose and Crown, disturbances in the kitchen date from early on.

Like Dennis, chef Michelle Martin would see a shape move past the doorway. It was always something caught out of the corner of her eye—too indistinct to identify. At times the presence seemed to enjoy a practical joke, Michelle recalled. "I'd be out back and [employee] Laurie would be out front. And she'd hear her name called and I'd hear my name called. One of us would say, 'I didn't call you, you called me.' And the other would answer, 'No, you called me!'"[6] Other employees have had similar experiences elsewhere in the building, suggesting that at least one of the ghosts has a sense of humour.

Who haunts the Rose and Crown? Apparently, the most active ghost is that of a little boy who is seen throughout the building.[7] He is certainly less than eight years old, and, according to local tales, was the son of a caretaker living in the attic. Although there are no accurate details concerning his clothing, he is a solid, lifelike apparition.

The ghost is so real that a server was once surprised to see a little boy peek out from a corner of the corridor behind the bar. Puzzled that a child could have walked so far into the Rose and Crown, she quickly made her way to where she had seen the little fellow. She had no doubt he would be there, for he had no place to go. Yet no one was there—he had simply vanished. She was unaware that two years earlier, a server had been down in the basement and seen a little boy peek out from behind a wall. During the years the site was a funeral home, bodies were prepared for viewing in this area, and the heavy concrete slabs that once supported the mortuary tables are still there.

Neighbours and passers-by on the street have reportedly
seen the silhouette of a little boy in this window.
COURTESY OF DIANE BELYK

From the time the pub was first opened, the boy has been
seen in the attic. Although after 1985 the attic has rarely been
used, passers-by on the street below have reported seeing a child
silhouetted in the small, top-floor window. From time to time
witnesses at a dance school and a hairdressing salon across the
street have reported seeing the dark outline of a boy's head in
the same location.

One of the strangest incidents happened about the mid-
1990s, when the employees, cleaning up after a party, put four
or five silver, helium-filled balloons in the hallway, where they
floated up to the ceiling. After closing time that night, Al Hunter
stood behind the bar while two other employees were sitting
on the high stools opposite him. As they relaxed, one person
noticed a party balloon suddenly appear. It floated toward them
until it was behind the bar where Al was standing. All three
people were surprised, because they believed that all of the

balloons had been stowed at the end of the hall. It was thought that this one must have escaped the attention of the employees during cleanup, and it was put back in the hall with the others.

After a few minutes Al and his co-workers caught sight of something at the entrance to the hall. As they watched, a balloon reached the middle of the door between the rooms, descended so that it was below the header, and then floated into the pub where it rose again, before coming to a stop behind the bar.

Among the three people in a reputedly haunted pub during the early hours of the morning, the idea that the floating balloon was somehow connected with ghosts was not entirely popular— there had to be a rational explanation. Someone suggested there must be a draft. But another person questioned why only *one* balloon would float in. Before he took the balloon by its string and returned it to the hall, Al took a felt pen and marked an *X* on it.

Minutes later, a balloon appeared in the passageway as before, and when it reached the bar, Al leaned forward and took it by the string. Clearly seen on one side of the silver orb was an *X*.

The balloon story created a stir among the employees of the Rose and Crown. The entity's obvious fascination with the balloon seemed to be in keeping with the actions of a small child.

That a little boy haunts the Rose and Crown was suggested by another occurrence. About 2007, after closing time, employees heard the sound of a bouncing ball upstairs. Recently this was repeated when employee Samantha McLellan was cleaning the third floor seating area, which is open only during peak periods. Because Tuesday afternoon is usually a quiet time, it has been set aside for washing the third floor. On this particular day she was busily scrubbing the tables when she heard what could not be mistaken for anything but a ball. "I heard it start to bounce in one corner," Samantha related, "and it went all across the room, and back. It was going back and forth, back and forth." It sounded as if it were a soft, air-filled rubber ball striking the floor and the walls. While the thumping noise probably did not last more than two minutes, it seemed much longer to the frightened employee. There is something disturbing about the third floor. Samantha, like Dennis, has also had the feeling of being watched while she has been alone there. "There's always that constant little feeling that someone is right there with you," she said.[8]

On the main floor, an incident occurred that even in the realm of the paranormal is rare. One of the regular patrons, a former policeman, would stop by for a beer while waiting for his wife. The man never expressed an interest in the ghostly stories associated with the pub, probably because like most police officers he was skeptical of anything that was less than solid evidence. However, one evening in 2005, he dropped into the Rose and Crown for a visit that would give him a glimpse into the past.

He had taken a place at the bar and ordered a beer from Dennis, and, as people often do, he turned in his seat to survey the patrons in the pub.

Dennis, who was busy behind the bar, was surprised when the customer suddenly asked, "What's that lady doing sitting over there?"

"What?" Dennis replied.

"Why is she sitting at that table?"

Dennis looked toward the bottom of the stairs, where he was pointing. No table was there. The man was known as a perfectly rational individual, so Dennis concluded he was joking.

Dennis was called away, but several minutes later, the policeman approached another bartender and again asked about the woman sitting at the table. He described a tall table covered by a white cloth. The person, he said, was wearing a long, pale grey dress and white gloves, her hair was done up on her head, and she was wearing a pillbox hat. Yet the pub had no tables of the type described by the patron, and no one else witnessed the scene.

The image had been so real that the man was unable to understand why no one else had seen it. Yet when it is recalled that the area was formerly the chapel, the sighting seems to make sense. The woman could have been sitting at the table that held the book of condolences signed by those attending a funeral. The pillbox hat she wore dates the service to the early 1960s.

Rather than a conscious haunting, the policeman was witnessing a residual event—a replay of part of a memorial service that may have taken place almost half a century earlier. These types of hauntings, in which the ghosts are reflections of the past, do occur, but what makes this phenomenon so unusual is that the patron saw not only the ghost, but also the condolence table. Moreover, why he saw this particular funeral, rather than the thousands of others that had taken place over the years, contributes to the mystery.

One of the ghosts haunting the Rose and Crown is not from the distant past but has a more recent history. Many of the pub employees believe that Chris, a young worker who died suddenly in 2006, remains on the premises. Chris was always a joker, and after his death he did not change. Dennis recalled:

> I'll be walking out to the trash can in the parking lot and I'll have the gate open, and I'll throw the trash in it and come walking back. And it won't be windy outside at all—not a gust of wind. When I walk back, just before I come through the gate, it slams shut. I'll just laugh and say, "Nice one, Chris."[9]

The gate incidents are common events that happen only to Dennis, who was particularly close to the young man. Even five years after Chris's death, Dennis still feels his presence at the Rose and Crown.

Although Samantha McLellan began work at the pub after Chris's passing and never knew him, she and other employees also sense that he is not far away. "There's always that feeling that Chris is right there," Samantha said, "always making sure everyone is doing what they should be doing."[10]

It is also possible that some of the ghosts predate even the funeral home. Samantha related a strange episode she witnessed. One night after the pub closed, the wife of a Calgary radio personality took cellphone photos throughout the building. In one of the photos snapped in the attic, weird images appeared. Shadowy shapes of a First Nations person, as well as individuals wearing clothes from before the building of the funeral home, could be seen. Apparently, several days after the pictures were taken, the photographer's cellphone burst into flames, and the digital images were lost.

Dennis has recently become general manager of the Rose and Crown and no longer works late nights, when most of the paranormal activity takes place. He remains the butt of Chris's practical jokes, though, when the gate at the side of the building slams in his face. He is philosophical about the haunting of the pub. "They're good ghosts," he said. "They were here before I was. They're letting me use their space and we all get along fine."[11]

HOSE AND HOUND

Although ghosts are never seen and only rarely heard at this pub on Ninth Avenue South East in the Inglewood district of Calgary, the Hose and Hound can be counted among that city's haunted pubs. The most active entity in the busy establishment is a jokester who enjoys playing tricks on the management and employees. The ghost, it seems, is a monkey named Barney.

The Hose and Hound occupies what was once Fire Station Number 3. The building, completed about 1907, had two bays that were designed to accommodate two fire engines, as well as stalls for the specially bred fire horses.

After Calgary's disastrous fire of 1886, all the city's fire halls were built of brick and sandstone. However, hay and oats for the horses, as well as the wooden stalls and the wood frame interior, were highly combustible. Not many years after the completion of the Ninth Avenue station, a fire broke out, gutting the horse stalls. The only casualty was Lightning, a horse that could not be led to safety in time. Calgary's fire chief, James "Cappy" Smart, had personally chosen this fine animal.[12]

Cappy Smart was a larger-than-life character who left his mark on the city. He was appointed Calgary's fire chief in 1898 and held that position until 1933. His forceful personality commanded respect at City Hall, with the result that Calgary was the first large centre in western Canada to acquire a gas-powered fire truck.

Cappy had a penchant for collecting exotic animals, which he distributed among Calgary's fire stations. Fire Station Number 3 was given a monkey named Barney. For the amusement of neighbourhood children on warm summer days, Barney was tied to a post in front of the fire hall.

Monkeys, though, rarely make good pets, for they are too clever to readily accept their confinement. Barney's temper was not improved by the teasing of either the firefighters or the children who visited him. His death came after he attacked a neighbourhood boy who had innocently offered him food. Barney had to be put down.

A monkey and a horse are among the ghosts
that haunt the Hose and Hound Pub.
COURTESY OF DIANE BELYK

By the early 1950s, longer engines were required to fight fires in Calgary's taller buildings, and the old station had become obsolete. It was opened as a pub in 1992 and, in 1996, Chuck Rose and his partner bought the business. The atmosphere of the Hose and Hound reflects the building's years as a fire hall: early firefighting equipment, as well as photos of Cappy Smart, illustrate the theme. Although no contemporary pictures of Barney are known to exist, it seems that the primate has remained behind to play his monkeyshines.

The one-time mascot creates his mischief in the kitchen, where the staff is particularly vulnerable to his tricks. In 1997, Chuck had his first encounter with Barney. One evening Chuck and chef Doug Brown were talking in the kitchen, standing about one and a half metres apart. To Chuck's right, about two metres off the floor, was a shelf with a pail of baking soda.[13] "Suddenly," Chuck recalled, "this four-litre pail flies between us,

Chuck Rose stands beside the shelves that once held the flying pail.

travels six feet over to the counter, and covers Doug with baking soda." Given the remote chance that vibrations from a passing train had led to the movement of the pail, the two men tried to duplicate it. "Yet every time we shook it off [the shelf] it just dropped. I have no idea what caused it."[14]

Two years later, Chuck, his wife, Elaine, and Dave, another chef, were standing in the kitchen when they were on the receiving end of another of Barney's tricks. As they were talking, the heavy-duty commercial dishwasher was off, with its loading tray out and the door open. The machine was designed to operate once the loaded tray was slid inside and could be turned on only when the door was tightly closed. Yet, without warning, the dishwasher came to life, spraying hot water on the three people in the kitchen. By the time they succeeded in closing the door, all three were soaked. The next day the service technician arrived. When they explained what had happened, he steadfastly maintained that, because of the safeguards built into the washer, such an accident was impossible. "Yet," Chuck concluded, "we know it happened."

Mike, who is now the kitchen manager and chef, witnessed the heavy oven door open and close three times before finally remaining open. Each time it closed with considerable force. On another occasion, one of the kitchen workers approached Chuck and said, "That monkey has been really busy this morning. I've had to retie my shoelaces twelve times."[15]

Not all incidents that take place involve Barney. Early in the morning, kitchen personnel have reported hearing the rapid clopping sound of a horse's hooves in the pub. The animal is not moving from one area of the pub to the other; it is restricted to one corner of the room. The fire horse, Lightning, is the likely source of the sounds. It is probably a residual haunting brought about by the horse's terrible end.

The behaviour of the pot-bellied stove on the upper floor is also puzzling. "You never see it, but it moves," Chuck said. "Sometimes when you leave at night it's at one place, and when you come back the next day, it's some place else." What is surprising is that the cast-iron object did not belong to the fire hall, but was added later, when decorators sought to recreate the turn-of-the-century atmosphere of the fire hall. It is not fixed in place and with much effort can be slid along the floor.[16]

The belief that a human presence also haunts the Hose and Hound began when former chef and now business partner Doug Brown arrived with a length of fire hose. With the help of his co-worker, Garry, he was planning to hang the hose high on the wall to hide the wires leading to the speakers. It was early in the morning and no one else was in the building. Doug had climbed the rungs of the ladder holding the hose, intent on securing it in place, when he was suddenly aware they were not alone. There was the sound of footsteps walking from the second-floor stairs and across the main floor. Garry heard it too. They both turned to see who it was, but as soon as they did, the footsteps stopped, and no one was there.

One morning after closing time, server Tanya and several staff members were seated at the bar, talking, when they heard the sound of the balls dropping on the pool table upstairs. The balls fall to the table by a mechanism that is activated when a player deposits a coin in the slot. The employees believed that a patron had remained in the building after the doors were locked. They quickly went upstairs to ask the customer to leave, but found nobody. Even more perplexing, there were no balls on either of the two pool tables. They had heard a very distinctive sound, one that is unlikely to be confused with anything else.

While some people have thought the human ghost was that of Cappy Smart, it seems unlikely, for the fire chief would have spent little time at one of the city's smaller fire halls. This ghost is a presence who is never seen. Given the tricks played on those unfortunate enough to be in the kitchen at the wrong time, it seems likely that it is Barney's ghost who does his monkey business at the Hose and Hound. There are no clues as to the identity of the other ghost.

THE CAT 'N FIDDLE

Calgary's Cat 'n Fiddle has many active ghosts. During the late hours after closing, the pub is positively creepy. Interestingly, when compared with most haunts, the building is relatively modern, dating to the middle of the twentieth century. Like the Rose and Crown, it began as a funeral parlour but served as one for only a little more than three decades.

The Biker, an apparition, and the full-throated rumble of a Harley-Davidson motorcycle are seen and heard in the Cat 'n Fiddle Pub.
COURTESY OF DIANE BELYK

Stuart McAllister, the current owner, has recreated a Scottish-style pub like the ones near his native country's famous golf courses. Golf memorabilia, brought in from Scotland, decorate the premises.

Rarely does a haunting encompass four of the five human senses, but this is the case at the Cat 'n Fiddle. The staff has seen, heard, smelled, and even felt the touch of ghosts. Ghostly activity, although happening all year, has its peak periods. The entities are particularly busy during the fall around Halloween, but not in December (which is frequently an energetic time at other haunts). January, though, is replete with paranormal occurrences, which sometimes number as many as three a day. Again in March, the ghosts are lively.

The basement is used for office space, a staff changing room, and a general storage area, and an uncomfortable feeling pervades this space. In some locations a person's skin may suddenly grow cold, and he or she may shiver involuntarily. It is not a place to linger even during the daylight hours.

During the time the building was a funeral home, most of the non-public activities took place downstairs, and reminders of that former business are in evidence today. A cold spot is present in the area now known as the green room, where two body fridges still exist. The McAllisters have never opened the coolers. Another cold spot is in the office that general manager Sheena McAllister shares with her mother, Jean. Some time ago, Jean was working at the computer in her office when she saw a human shadow move past her desk. She was so upset that she refused to return to the basement for the rest of the day.

One of the earliest stories goes back to the pub's first years, when one of the servers arrived for work following a night on the town and asked to have a few minutes alone until she felt better. She was sitting on the couch in the basement, away from the noise of the pub, when she felt arms around her, soft and comforting. Almost instantly, her headache was gone.

The entity offering consolation might be the famous Woman in Red, who is said to have had a connection to the building when it was a funeral home. She could have been a person who often dealt with families suffering personal loss. As an apparition, she has been seen behind the bar and in the basement, which contains the room where embalming once took place. She is usually only glimpsed, but on several occasions Sheena has witnessed something more. "I've never seen her face," she said. "I just see her red dress and her legs. The dress goes to the knees and she has high heels on."[17] Interestingly, the appearance of the

Woman in Red is accompanied by a pungent rose perfume.

About 2001, Randy, a cook who works at the Cat 'n Fiddle, was in the basement changing his shoes when he saw a woman whom he thought was Jean walk past him. He noticed only the lower part of her body, including her red dress, nylons, and high-heeled shoes that made a click, click, click sound on the concrete floor. A short time later when he was upstairs, he saw Jean but was shocked to discover her dress was blue.

While it has been said that the Woman in Red managed the funeral parlour, her dress and shoes hardly fit that profession. Unlike similar funeral homes, there were no living quarters attached, so the dress and shoes would have been worn only during her off-hours.

Another ghost haunting the Cat 'n Fiddle is the Biker. Tall and slim, with short dark hair, and wearing a full leather motorcycle outfit, he appears only briefly. In the early hours of the morning, when he is usually seen, employees will often hear what appears to be a big Harley-Davidson motorcycle. Strangely, the sound does not seem to come from the street, but from above the building—as if the motorcycle were on the roof.

Long after closing time, cook Matt Gagat and a former employee, Shane, were sitting at a table near the wall. All the doors were locked, the lights were turned down, and they were minutes away from leaving when they happened to glance at a picture on the wall. Reflected in the glass was a tall, slim figure. Knowing that the building was secure, both men were surprised. They turned in the direction of the reflection, but no living person was there. Although shaken at the time, Matt put the incident in context: "You hear that a lot of things happen, so I'm getting used to it."[18]

A third sighting may reflect the time when the building served as a funeral home. The spectre is a tall man, wearing a formal morning suit and a black silk top hat, which was the traditional garb of an undertaker. He is a solid apparition that is often mistaken for a living person. Frequently he gives male patrons a shock, for when they enter the men's restroom, they see a full-bodied apparition in strange clothing standing by the sinks. Believing that he is a real person, the patrons go about their business only to witness the man suddenly walk through the wall. Many men have related their accounts of the ghost to the bartenders and servers.

On the other side of the wall is the dart room, where the ghost appears and then disappears almost immediately. The restroom was added during renovations, so no wall would have separated the two rooms before it was a pub. When the building was a funeral home, the areas that are now the dart room and restroom were part of a closed space within the chapel, where family members could grieve privately. The ghost's formal attire and his walk through the wall may suggest that he is a recording from the past, repeating the routine he had performed in life.[19] He would have entered to seat occupants in this room and then to escort them out.

A cat is also among the ghosts haunting this Calgary pub. Going down the back stairs, Sheena, out of the corner of her eye, often caught sight of a dark brown or grey feline. "It's like I'm about to step on the poor thing, but when I look down it's not there."[20] According to a psychic brought in by a Calgary paranormal group, there is a family of cats living in the basement. It would have been common practice to keep these animals on the premises to control vermin.

Psychics have maintained that, in addition to the three spectres, other ghosts, unseen by the staff and patrons, haunt the pub. Given the broad range of phenomena at the Cat 'n Fiddle, this is likely.

The women's restroom is one of the scenes of an event that apparently severely frightened an unwelcome visitor. In the early hours of the morning, after the last employee had left, a thief broke into the Cat 'n Fiddle and began searching for cash. The event, which was caught on security tape, added another dimension to the pub haunting. While there was no sound on the tape, the burglar's actions told an interesting story. As he prowled the premises, it was clear something was disturbing him. He stopped abruptly and turned his head, as though listening to something. Then he moved toward the women's restroom. Obviously something in there continued to bother him. Sheena recalled:

> He kept going to the ladies' bathroom. So right away we knew that the ghosts were fooling with him. Then he was opening the door at the front. On the camera when you slow it down you can see orbs around the door. By this time he had the money and grabbed a bottle of Baileys [Irish Cream whiskey]. Something happened that must have been horrific, because he actually took two steps back, dropped the Baileys, and then ran out the door.

"The ghosts are very protective of us," she concluded. Unfortunately the burglar was never caught, so it is impossible to know what the ghost or ghosts did to produce such fear.

When head server Heather Herfft began working at the Cat 'n Fiddle, she made a pact with the ghosts that if they did not bother her, she would not bother them. To some extent they have kept their side of the bargain. In fact, she also felt the ghosts have been protective of her.

Heather recalled that in 2003 she arrived early one morning

to do paperwork. While she and Chief, the cook, were alone in the building, an electrician arrived to test the fire panel. At the time, the pub had an old-fashioned Wurlitzer-style jukebox, the top of which was clear glass that exposed the metal-framed pages. On the pages were typed the titles of the songs that customers could select, and the pages could be turned from the front of the jukebox. The cook was standing in front of the Wurltizer when the electrician entered. As the electrician crossed the room, footsteps echoed on the floor behind him. At the same time, without being touched, the pages in the jukebox began to turn slowly. Heather believed that this ghostly action was prompted by the arrival of the electrician when the Cat 'n Fiddle was closed. The entity was letting the man know he was trespassing where strangers ought to tread carefully.

As mentioned elsewhere, ghosts have the ability to interfere with electrical wiring and the operation of sophisticated electronic devices. At the beginning of one shift, whenever Heather rang in her order, the computer screen consistently showed "pizza and Corona [beer]." This happened only to Heather, and not to any of the other servers. Moreover, the Cat 'n Fiddle did not sell pizza at the time, so the item would have had to be added to the menu by someone who had administrative privileges for the computer, and Heather was busy on the floor. Annoyed, she finally asked the ghost to stop because she could not get her work done. From then on, the orders she punched in were right.

Occasionally, it is clear that the ghosts in the electronics are intent on only one thing—creating mischief. At times, during major sporting events such as the Stanley Cup, Grey Cup, and Super Bowl, one or more of the entities seems intent on disrupting the games on the big-screen televisions by turning on a cartoon channel. Usually this is a petty irritation that occurs once or twice during an event. However, one day, the entity was determined to create a disturbance. Because the commercials are much louder than the game, Sheena held the remote-control wands in her hand so she could press the mute buttons.

It is not difficult to imagine the feelings of the customers when the channel on the television changed from the big game to *Sponge Bob SquarePants*. And of course, Sheena was holding the channel changers. "I'm not doing this, you guys," Sheena pleaded, and passed the controls to someone else. It made no difference, for once the game was on, the channels switched back to cartoons. Frustrated beyond endurance, she turned the channels back to the game, took the batteries out of the controllers, and said, "Okay, you guys, now do it!" Suddenly, every screen returned to a cartoon channel.

Although the entity or entities performed before a room full of sports fans, mischievous ghosts will often single out one person as the target of their tricks. Because no one else is aware of the incident, the victim is reluctant to come forward. In one case, though, there was a witness. "I have a story that I wouldn't dare to repeat if I didn't have someone else there to verify it," admitted Heather. One day, when she came to work, she brought her purse with her and stored it in a cubbyhole beside the desk in her office. When she left, she made sure the door was locked and her purse was safe. At the end of her shift she returned to her office to pick up her purse, but the cubbyhole was empty. Puzzled, because she was the only employee with a key to her door, she looked everywhere in the room. Thinking that she might have left it in her car, Heather went to the parking lot and searched it without success. She recalled:

I think it's got to be in the office, so I go back and open the cubbyhole again and search all through it and I can't find it. So I go get Lisa, one of my other waitresses, and say, "I've lost my purse, come help me find it." So she comes down and she looks through the cupboard as well and we search the whole office, and we can't find it at all. I say to Lisa, "Maybe I'll check my vehicle one more time." She says, "Maybe you'd better ask [the ghosts] for it back." I close and lock my door and say, "Hey guys, can I have my purse back now?" I go back and check the vehicle, and it's nowhere. I come back to my office and open it up, and open up the cubbyhole and [my purse is] right there![21]

Heather's missing purse was a personal experience, but other implements used at the bar often disappear until the staff asks for them back. Then, within a few minutes, the tools will return to their accustomed place.

Sounds that are not connected to sightings are a common feature of the Cat 'n Fiddle haunting. Soft, indistinct voices have been heard in the pub, but in one case, the voices were anything but quiet. In the early hours one morning, before going home, Sheena and one of her employees decided to play a video game. As she put the money in the slot, what sounded like an argument between a man and a woman broke out in the adjoining room. "It started getting louder and louder, but you just couldn't hear what they were saying. It sounded like they were angry."[22] She was amazed, for the doors had been locked, and there were only the two of them in the building. The cacophony reached its climax when, as Sheena related, "Suddenly there was a huge bang in the dart room. I mean huge!" Then there was silence. After checking the dart room and finding no one there, and nothing out of place, they thought it might be best to leave.

At least one of the ghosts at the Cat 'n Fiddle seemed to form an attachment to particular employees. On several occasions an entity has accompanied servers home after work. Heather Herfft, who usually takes her bike to work and then accepts a ride home from fellow employees, feels that the ghosts are only being protective. If it is a new employee who drives her home, a ghost is likely to play the role of chaperone.

At her home, though, the presence is at least an overnight guest. "Because it's your house and so much smaller a space," Heather stated, "you notice it, and feel it that much more. You know how it is when you're sitting watching television and you know someone's there."[23]

Heather did not want to raise the matter with her husband, Kelly, so she kept to herself the fact that they had a ghost visitor. However, one evening all that changed when she was lounging on the couch and Kelly was sitting on a living room chair. As the restless ghost paced back and forth at the back of the room, she did her best to ignore it, but Kelly was becoming increasingly agitated. Finally, he shouted, "What the hell's going on behind me?" He, too, had sensed the restless presence in the room.

As often happens in pubs like the Cat 'n Fiddle where there is a low staff turnover, ghosts may object to employees resigning. In 2009, after working at the pub for eight years, Lisa was serving her last shift. As she was leaving through the kitchen, a knife came off the wall and flew by, just missing her. Upset, she continued downstairs to change. As she reached the basement, a light bulb above her head suddenly burst. Ghosts may not like change, and the anger of this entity was unmistakable.

Unlike the ghostly hug experienced by one of the servers, not all physical contact has been well intentioned. In 2008, Sheena was the recipient of an action that, had it been done by a living person, would have been regarded as flippant and familiar, yet done by something from beyond the grave, it was abhorrent and terrifying. "I was walking downstairs and I had my hair down and they literally lifted it up. I was *petrified*."[24] This unwanted behaviour typifies a younger man. While it seems the Biker may be the chief suspect, pubs are known to attract other young male ghosts, people who have died in the vicinity.

On at least one occasion, the ghost behaved with a malice that is rare in a haunting. Glasses at the pub are known to fly off the wooden rail above the bar without inflicting personal injury, but once, one of them struck a person. In June of 2011, Gabby, a bartender, was working behind the counter when a glass flew off the shelf and struck her on the knee. It flew with such force that it shattered, cutting her knee so badly that it required stitches.

After closing time, bottles of liquor have been known to come off the shelves and barstools propelled across the floor. Perhaps ghosts are impatient to have the living leave so that they can have the building to themselves. "We have the strangest things happen here—everyone says they're impossible," Sheena McAllister asserted, "but they do." It is easy to agree with her, for the Cat 'n Fiddle ranks among not only Calgary's, but North America's most haunted pubs.

Few cities can claim three paranormally active pubs. Yet the Rose and Crown, the Hose and Hound, and the Cat 'n Fiddle each have had their share of well-documented occurrences. Calgary is one city where a night on the town may lead to an evening beyond anything that one might expect.

MAIN STREET INN

Although the little community of Gravelbourg, Saskatchewan, has a population of only slightly more than a thousand people, it has more than its share of ghosts. The Historic Bishops Residence, mentioned earlier, is not the only haunt. Many residents believe that a former convent, which has been turned into apartments, has more than one ghost. Occasionally, renters will be disturbed by three knocks on their door and, when they answer the summons, no one will be there. One ghost is apparently very prim and is known to become upset when any of the tenants use "improper" language. After this happens, things will be thrown about the apartment by unseen hands.

Several blocks away from the former convent is the Main Street Inn. Once known as the Ambassador Hotel, the old building is now almost exclusively a bar. It too is haunted. The resident ghost is believed to be Walter, a long-time occupant of the inn who died in his room on the second floor many years ago.

Barbara Mercer, who worked at the bar for six years until 2010, had many unusual experiences. Walter, like many ghosts, appears to enjoy manipulating electronics. "I'd be sitting here late at night before closing and the television would turn off or the jukebox would turn on," Barbara recalled. "The house stereo, which is always on CD, one time came on, and it was the radio, and the song that it was playing was 'It's Only Magic.'"[25]

At night, whenever Barbara had to go to the storage room at the rear of the bar, she experienced a strange feeling. "I would always feel that there was somebody right behind me—like they were following me."

Walter's activities are not confined to the lower floor. "Anybody who's ever stayed in the rooms above [the bar] say it's really haunted," Barbara said. "I myself would never sleep up there."

The bar of the Main Street Inn is haunted
by the ghost of a former hotel resident.
COURTESY OF DIANE BELYK

Barbara's daughter, Scarlett, began working in the bar in 2010 and has also experienced the phantom. "The jukebox turns on and off umpteen times and I hear him walking upstairs."[26] So common are these events that virtually every employee who has ever worked at the bar has experienced them. Although long dead, Walter continues to make his presence known at the Main Street Inn.

At night, the east wing of Crease Clinic can be more frightening
than some of the horror movies that have been shot there.

CHAPTER SIX

HAUNTED HOSPITALS

CREASE CLINIC: SADNESS, TEARS, TERROR, AND GHOSTS

Ironically, the old psychiatric institution Essondale, later called Riverview Hospital, in Coquitlam closed its doors on Friday, the thirteenth of July, 2012. The date was appropriate, for Essondale was never a place for the lucky. The crude treatments administered to its patients during most of its history were little better than barbaric, and it is no wonder that the old buildings are haunted.

Some of the happenings have been associated with the three large main buildings that stand on the crest of a low hill overlooking the Fraser River flood plain: West Lawn, Centre Lawn, and East Lawn. Crease Clinic stands apart from them, at the bottom of a slope just above the Lougheed Highway. Birds nesting in the attic or homeless people gaining entrance explain some of the activity in the abandoned buildings, but not all occurrences can be as easily dismissed. The haunting of the three old buildings at the top of the hill is discussed in *Ghosts: More Eerie Encounters*, yet the most active haunting has occurred in Crease Clinic, the smallest of the four buildings.

Nowhere in the hospital complex was a more frightening place than Crease Clinic (later Crease Unit): many well-documented accounts of paranormal events are associated with this building. The first section of it was completed in 1934 as a treatment facility for shell-shocked veterans of the First World War. A mirror wing was begun after the Second World War, and the combined facility was opened in 1949 as the Crease Clinic of Psychological Medicine. Intended to be an acute-care facility for patients requiring only short hospital stays, it was regarded as using the most modern of treatment techniques.[1]

By the late 1960s, however, mental health treatment was being decentralized, and the facility had no place in the new model. In 1992 Crease Clinic closed as a treatment facility, and gradually the structure was allowed to fall into disrepair.

The worn carpets disintegrated on the floors and the paint peeled from the walls, but the terrible pain suffered by so many patients over the years seemed to have seeped into the plaster of the dayrooms, dorms, and side rooms—the narrow, two-by-three-metre cells that confined troubled souls.

One of the first reported paranormal events at Crease took place while the facility was still operating as a psychiatric hospital. Like the elevator in the large brick building to the north, one of the two lifts in the building seemed to be haunted. While the entity that occupied the other elevator was more mischievous than malevolent (in keeping with poltergeist activity), Crease's east wing elevator passengers were frequently taken on an unpleasant and unpredictable ride from floor to floor. In some cases the riders complained of feeling nauseated and depressed.

After Crease was closed, a number of movie and television companies, including Ten Thirteen Productions, makers of *The X-Files*, filmed in the building. Some of the productions filmed at Crease were low-budget horror films that were in keeping with the depressing atmosphere that hung over the building. For the men and women connected with the film industry, Crease was more than simply a film location—it carried a heaviness that weighed down on the casts and crews.

"Just thinking of that place makes me anxious. It is not a friendly place, it does not have good vibes, it is dark where there is light, it left me freezing cold in the middle of summer," said production assistant Corinna Carlson. "I would never ever work there again."[2] But because the provincial government rented the building at such a low price, few film companies were likely to look elsewhere for a similar site in the Vancouver area.

A visit to the Crease building left a well-trained police dog clearly frightened. In 2002, a dangerous patient missing from another building and a broken window at Crease prompted a call to the Royal Canadian Mounted Police (RCMP), which brought in a police dog and handler. The dog would not pass beyond the entrance to the building, even at the firm urging of her handler. Eventually two police officers searched the building themselves without finding an intruder. In the end, the window was simply boarded up.

Gordon Juli did not believe in ghosts when he came to Vancouver from the Okanagan in 1992, that is, he didn't until 1997 when he began working security for the film industry at Crease Clinic. One of the first pieces of advice Gordon received from his supervisor concerned not only the haunted elevator, but also the supposedly innocuous second passenger lift. Unless he was carrying a cellphone or walkie-talkie with a contact on the other end, Gordon was told, "Don't use them because these elevators have a mind of their own."

Later, both lifts and their panels were removed, and the power was turned off to the shafts. Yet even without power, the strange movements of the elevators continued. Production companies would arrive at Crease to find an elevator door on one or another of the floors wide open, exposing the gaping shaft. This was such a common event that the BC Buildings

Corporation (BCBC), on behalf of the provincial government, placed boards across the entrances to all the elevator doors.

Gordon had an opportunity to witness the bizarre behaviour of one of the ghost elevators for himself. Not long after the elevators were removed, Gordon was making rounds of the building. He covered the second floor, walking past the elevator on the east wing and down the corridor. All appeared normal until he got to the far end of what was once Ward East 2. Although the building had a steam heating system, which did not create drafts, as Gordon approached the end of the hall, he walked into a shaft of cold air. What was disconcerting for him was that around the area of the cold spot were thousands of dead ladybugs. "I've never in my life seen two [dead] ladybugs together. Now there were thousands of them." On his return, Gordon continued up the hall until he reached the east side elevator. Suddenly, to his amazement the doors slid open, revealing a black pit behind a wooden barrier. Only after reporting the incident to his supervisor did Gordon learn why BCBC had barricaded the elevator doors.

The Crease dining hall, although not generally connected with paranormal activity, was the scene for at least one ghost story. Built with banks of large windows to let in plenty of light, the second-floor, cafeteria-style dining rooms, serving patients and staff separately, were perfect locations for some film projects. In 2004, a company began filming in the dining room. Because the script required special effects, a new lavatory was built right next to the women's restroom. To complete the job, a member of the construction crew took the cubicles from the original women's restroom. At the end of the day, and unknown to the film company, one of the construction crew went into the building to finish some work.

By the time he reached the door to leave, the man was

surprised that while he had one key to let himself out by a smaller lock, the main exit door had been locked by a master key. Later, the security staff steadfastly maintained that they had not set the big universal lock. The construction worker could not leave the building through the main entrance, so only one other exit was available: the fire door. A brass pressure bar had been installed to open the fire door without fail. In the midst of thick smoke, the slightest touch on the bar would easily open the heavy steel portal, offering a sure escape route for anyone trapped inside. The worker pressed on the cool, smooth brass handle. Nothing happened. Despite his repeated attempts to open the door, the handle would not budge. Without a cellphone, the crew member spent an unpleasant night. After being freed the next morning, he tried the fire door and it opened without difficulty. The prisoner of the dining hall was the member of the construction crew who had removed the cubicles from the restroom—one might speculate that the ghost resented these changes.

There was another weird event during the filming of a movie a number of years ago. The crew had planned to set up meal catering on Ward East 2, and when security arrived early that morning to check out the location, they found a large amount of water on the floor. Gordon Juli's first thought was that it had come from a burst water pipe. However, there were no pipes in the floor, ceiling, or walls, and the roof did not leak. "It was just like there was a big puddle."

Mark Tuit was the producer and director of the low-budget horror picture *Subhuman*, and in 2003, arriving very early one morning, he let himself in with one of the few keys given out by the building management. He intended to plan the day's shooting, and was probably somewhat preoccupied as he walked down the long corridor leading to a ward. He later remarked, "I hear what sounds like footsteps." Believing that it was probably the production company's security guard, Tuit waited; he did not want to surprise the guard. It was dark, and the filmmaker could see only a few metres ahead of him. Off the main corridor was another wing from which the footsteps seemed to be coming. As the sound increased in volume, he expected that the guard would turn the corner into the main hallway where the filmmaker stood. No one appeared. Then the footsteps stopped. "Then from behind me three ceiling tiles crash to the floor. I freeze, terrified to turn around. I begin breathing again and slowly back out of the building."[3] During the shooting of his film, Tuit never returned alone to the building.

Among the strange and irritating phenomena to plague producers filming at Crease Clinic in 1993 were the "rogue lights." In their contracts with BCBC, production companies were responsible for turning off all the lights on the set at the end of the day. This job fell to the locations crew, but they came to realize the task was often difficult or impossible. As the crew turned off one light bank, another would be mysteriously turned on. The entire exercise would continue for up to an hour until the crew finally gave up. By 2002, the production companies simply left the lights on. Given the cost of labour, it was too expensive to do otherwise, and eventually BCBC agreed to absorb the extra cost of the phantom lights.

During location shooting at Crease, film security personnel usually did not have to enter the building; they patrolled only the perimeter. However, some productions required special equipment, and the building's fire alarm had to be turned off around the clock. Under these conditions, security staff had to go inside the former institution, checking each floor. Not all employees, though, would go beyond the entrance to Crease.

Even perimeter patrols could be scary. In 2004 Gordon Juli

was sitting in his car in the driveway that separated the Crease building from the dining hall. Suddenly, the quiet of the evening was broken by a piercing scream that seemed to freeze the blood in his veins. The terrible sound appeared to come from the brow of the hill, east of what once was the Essondale post office and small store. Gordon searched the area but couldn't find anything.

The "phantom scream" was a frightening event experienced by hospital staff many years before. It was said to have been the cry of a woman murdered while walking from the bus stop in front of the post office to one of the buildings.

When patrolling the perimeter of Crease, Gordon's shift partner once saw a dark figure move past the windows on Ward East 3. No intruder could be found, but Gordon's colleague was positive that he had seen a dark figure silhouetted in the windows.

From the beginning, production companies have constructed elaborate sets—decorative archways, a prison cellblock, even a large furnished apartment—that have not been pulled down after filming, but have been used later by other companies.

In 2003 Gordon Juli took his girlfriend on a tour of the building. When they reached the apartment set on the third floor, they sat down on the couch. As they moved closer together, they suddenly heard a woman's voice. It was a low whisper, so faint that neither Gordon nor his girlfriend could make out the words. Seconds later the whisper was repeated, leaving the couple to shake their heads. What is particularly interesting is that they identified a woman's voice: for many years the area where the set is located was exclusively a female ward.

Several weeks later, while doing perimeter patrol, Gordon had reason to use the restroom. The nearest operating toilet was on the second floor in Crease. He entered the building, climbed the stairs, and locked the lavatory door behind him.

Several minutes had passed when the eerie silence of the building was broken by a sharp knock on the door. He was aware that there should not have been anyone else in the building, but there was no mistaking the knock. He opened the door but no one was in sight.

Gordon began a search of the building. He found nothing unusual on the lower floors, but when he reached the third floor and searched the apartment set he had visited earlier, he heard the same low female whisper. Again, it was impossible to understand the words. On the fourth floor, the silence was broken by a sound similar to a whooping cough. He found nothing untoward in the east or west wings of the fourth floor and so continued up to the attic. Other than supporting posts, this was a completely open space. The fluorescent lights were all on, although the area was rarely visited, and he had a good view of the entire attic. On entering, he heard the sound of someone running way, but there was not another living soul in the room. A thorough search revealed nothing. Shaken, Gordon decided it was time to leave.

However, the night wasn't over. As he sat in his car facing the entrance to the building, he observed a shadowy figure walk down the hall in the direction of the glass doors in front of him. The hallway was only a few feet long, but Gordon had time to observe the human shape. Then, as it reached the doors, it disappeared.

Although films continue to be made there, Crease and the other buildings will soon be torn down. The ghosts of the old psychiatric hospital will have to find new places to haunt.

BROOKS: THREE GHOSTS

In Alberta, the Brooks Community Cultural Centre is counted as one of the province's most haunted locations. The building began as a hospital, and typically, places where sudden deaths occur have their share of ghosts. Yet according to legend, as well as witnesses, here it is not only patients but also staff that remain earthbound.

Brooks is a bustling community on the Trans-Canada Highway, a little less than two hundred kilometres southeast of Calgary. Construction of the Brooks Hospital began in 1942, and it opened the following year. Some forty years later, a new health care facility was built, and the old hospital was closed. The building was renovated and, to serve its new role as a community college, a new wing was added. In the fall of 1991, the college moved to a new campus, and the former hospital became the Brooks Centre. The building also houses the Brooks Boys and Girls Club, a daycare facility, preschool, food bank, and pottery guild on its two levels.

Most of the ghost stories relate to the lower floor of the old building. One tale concerns an older man in a white lab coat, carrying a clipboard, who has been seen standing in the hospital wing. Another tells of a small boy with a backpack who is also supposed to be seen there. The child seems confused and says that he is lost.[4]

Moe Andruschak, associate director of the Support, Prevent, Educate, Counsel Association for Children and Families (SPEC), had her office around the corner from the children's playroom. Often her daughter and young granddaughter would stop by to see her, and later she would accompany them to the playroom where there were many toys to amuse the little girl.

One day in 2008, the eighteen-month-old child and her mother stopped by Moe's office. After a short visit, Moe and her daughter walked down the hall toward the playroom as the toddler ran ahead. When she reached the corner where the old wing branched off, she stopped suddenly and faced the playroom.

She bent slightly forward, placed her hands on her knees, and began addressing someone hidden around the corner. The child was so animated that both women were sure that, in the babbling fashion of her age group, she was speaking to someone who had come from the playroom. When they reached the spot, though, only the toddler stood in the hallway.

Once, soon after Glenda Coombs began working at the Brooks Centre daycare in the summer of 2004, she was assigned to the three- and four-year-old children's room. Following a morning when the children had played with the toys in their room, Glenda decided to take them outdoors to enjoy the pleasant weather. Before leaving she made sure all the toys were put back in their proper place and the room was tidy. However, Glenda recalled, "When I came back, the entire room was in shambles—the toys were all over the place."[5] Glenda questioned the other staff members, but no one had entered the area.

Shortly after that first experience, when Glenda was in the same room, the lights abruptly went out. Only when the breaker was reset was the room illuminated again. There was seemingly no reason why the electrical circuit would have been tripped.

If these were the only events she experienced, Glenda might have forgotten them. As she discovered, however, they were only the harbingers of what was to come.

One day, when Glenda was reading to the youngest children at the daycare, she heard a voice that chilled her to the core. It said, "I'm a baby, play with me." The sound came from the area containing the toys. Although there were many plush toys in the room that talked when they were hugged or squeezed, none of them were programmed to say the words Glenda heard. Even more frightening was the fact that it was not the typical childlike voice of a toy, but the deep bass tones of a man. Glenda was the only adult in the room at the time.

The former site of the Brooks Hospital is still haunted
by many ghosts associated with its past.
COURTESY OF DIANE BELYK

"Fred," as the ghost on the lower floor is called, is an active
presence. One of his favourite tricks is to knock toys off the
racks. Because the items are neatly shelved, there is no chance
that they might fall off on their own, but every week or two,
a toy drops from the shelf to the floor. Fred, it should be
mentioned, is not a malicious ghost. He has always avoided
frightening the children and makes himself known only to the
daycare personnel.

He was once glimpsed by Rachael, a former worker, who
described him as being a tall, imposing figure. Glenda also

saw Fred when she was walking past the area where children were cared for before and after school. The room should have been unoccupied at the time, and she was surprised to glimpse someone standing there. When she turned to look, it was clear that the figure was not human. "He was very tall with big broad shoulders," Glenda remembered.[6] Although he looked solid, the form was dark and featureless—like a three-dimensional shadow.

The ghost is not limited to one room, although he is most active in the area assigned to the young children. One day in 2010, when none of the children were at the daycare, Glenda and a fellow employee, Berlynn, left the audio monitor on in the room. Suddenly, over the speaker system, they heard heavy breathing. However, the deep, rhythmic, rasping sounds abruptly stopped when Glenda entered the room to investigate.

Another male ghost is said to haunt the centre. On one occasion, in 2005, a staff member was attempting to scan several photos taken in the foyer, but the scanner refused to operate. This was surprising since it had worked perfectly the day before. Frustrated, the woman went home during her lunch hour and brought in her own scanner. Still the computer screen indicated an equipment failure. The next day a third scanner was obtained; it produced similar results, except something did appear on the screen. On the file name line was the word *George*, the name of a hospital janitor who is thought to haunt the building. The person who had scanned in the pictures had left that line blank—there is no way to explain how the name appeared.

With limited communication between the agencies and groups that use the Brooks Centre, it may be that Fred, the daycare ghost, is actually George, the cigar-smoking janitor.

He is most active on the lower floor of the old hospital wing, but makes his presence known throughout much of the facility.

As with all entities, George does not like changes to his haunt, so when two young workers from Calgary arrived in 2009 to increase the size of the games room, they were aware that George might make his objections known. The workers had earlier heard stories of the haunting of the centre, but were not aware of what parts were affected. "I told them," employee Adele Christen recalled, "that people had noticed things down here [where they were working], but if you do it's okay, because the ghosts are all friendly."[7]

Over the years there had been earlier renovations, and one of the walls, where a new door was planned, had two layers of drywall. As the men pulled the first layer away, they were shocked to discover that one piece of gypsum board contained a pencil sketch of a long, lanky young man with chin stubble—a striking image of one of the workers who had discovered the drawing. What was so chilling was that the figure wore a Stetson, a hat typically worn by the worker. On this day, though, he had left it at home in Calgary. The man was so shaken that before leaving for lunch, he tossed the piece of wallboard into the big waste container.

On their return that afternoon, they found an old piece of hospital blanket where they had been working. The only explanation was that it had been secured for many years between the two layers of drywall, but they had not noticed it when they removed that section. Further, it was lying on top of a pile of debris where they should have seen it earlier. Believing that the blanket must have had some significance beyond their understanding, employees of the centre placed it between the studs, to be sealed again within the new layer of drywall. Such bizarre happenings appear to be in keeping with George's odd behaviour—odd even for a ghost.

Moe Andruschak believes the ghost janitor is also very active on the second floor of the building. In 2003, she had an appointment in her office with an employee from an organization that shared space in the Brooks Centre. By nature the man was very emotional. During their meeting his voice boomed so loud that it almost seemed to shake the building, and as he spoke, he moved his arms in every direction. Some distance behind his chair, which faced Moe's desk, was a filing cabinet angled into one corner of the room. On top of the cabinet was a glass-framed picture, partially hidden by a candle and several other decorative objects.

As he continued talking loudly and gesticulating, Moe saw the picture levitate about a quarter of a metre above the cabinet, move over the candle and other objects, and crash to the floor. The man, who had his back to the cabinet, had no idea what had happened. He was obviously shaken by the loud noise behind him, and in answer to his look of surprise Moe said, "You really must have woken up George."[8] Despite the distance to the floor, the glass in the frame was not broken. Also, the things in front of the picture remained undisturbed. After the incident the man's behaviour was much more subdued, Moe recalled.

In November 2010, as was their usual practice, Boys and Girls Club team leader Janna Grant and youth coordinator Melissa Melindi remained behind to tidy up after the daily program was over. On this day Marley, a student staff volunteer, was helping them. Their last task before leaving was to clean the kitchen where the children had explored their culinary skills. The room opened to an outside door leading to a wrought-iron fire escape. When anyone stood on a stair, the weight produced an unmistakable clinking sound as the metal moved slightly.

As they went about their chores, Janna recalled, "We heard pounding on that door, and it was so loud that it's impossible to replicate."[9] There were four or five loud thumps that frightened them, and no one wanted to approach the door. "We just sat there and froze." After several seconds Janna concluded that it must be someone from the centre who had a heavy load to carry in from the parking lot below the fire escape. The fire door would have been the easiest entry.

Janna had taken several steps toward the door when two more loud thumps reverberated in the room. She pressed down on the brass latch and the door opened. To her amazement, no one stood in the doorway, and she could see that there was no one below on the fire escape. Melissa and Marley ran to the windows that overlooked the parking lot. Although it was growing dark, there was enough light to see that not a soul was there either.

Later, when they had time to consider their experience, it occurred to them that the only sound they had heard was the pounding on the door. It could not be easily explained for, as Janna judged, "The stairs are old and if somebody had run up, knocked, and run down, you'd hear them." Also, Janna had opened the door immediately after the last two knocks, so there was really no time for anyone to escape.

It has long been speculated that the women's restroom on the second floor is haunted—some people feel the presence is that of a child who died in the hospital. Indeed, Moe Andruschak, who has worked at the centre since the year 2000, recalls that at least one person a number of years ago saw the ghost of a little girl playing in the restroom. No sightings have occurred recently, but there is certainly something strange about the room.

Because the employees from the Boys and Girls Club are the last to leave, they ensure that all of the windows in the

Before three witnesses, an unseen presence
rapped loudly on this fire escape door.
COURTESY OF DIANE BELYK

public rooms on the second floor are shut. Several years ago, when the morning staff arrived, one small window in the restroom was often open. Many people simply assumed that the last staff members leaving the building had not checked the lavatory. However, the same restroom window being open became such a common event that it could not be readily dismissed as human error.

Janna Grant was particularly shaken when, one evening, she had secured all the windows and later remembered taking special care to lock the small window in the women's restroom. On this occasion, Janna recalled, she had remained in the building later than usual:

> I was across the hall [from the restroom] in my supervisor's office getting my evaluation, and I had to use the bathroom so I popped across the hall. When I got up and went across, my supervisor could actually hear me scream. The window was wide open again. After I finished my evaluation, we checked, and the window was open again!

Eventually, the city of Brooks, which maintains the centre, solved the problem by bolting the frame permanently shut.

The restroom itself frequently gives the second-floor staff an uncomfortable feeling. Often, water is splashed over the counter and floors. While it is easy to blame the younger children of the Boys and Girls Club, such incidents occur at times when they are not on the premises. Moreover, the children dislike this restroom. "They say they find the bathroom scary," Janna observed, "or that they don't like it." Such feelings have nothing to do with the appearance of the room, which is bright and well maintained, and overlooks a park.

While the little boy with the backpack and the man in the white lab coat do not seem to be active, the ghost of George the janitor and the little girl in the restroom continue to make themselves known. At the Brooks Centre, it seems that the shades of the past reach into the present.

ROYAL COLUMBIAN: THE WAKER

In Canada's Western provinces, as elsewhere, ghosts sometimes remain long-term residents in the acute-care hospitals where they took their last breath. One such institution is New Westminster's Royal Columbian Hospital, a major health care facility in British Columbia. Although the Columbia Tower is a fairly recent addition to the hospital—it was completed in the 1990s—it has become known as the source of ghostly activity. On Ward South 3, one room has gained an unsettling reputation. It is the spot where night-shift staff frequently spend their breaks, taking brief naps. During the twelve-hour work periods, as the nurses doze in the comfortable chairs in the room, they are often awakened by what feels like a hand pressing on their shoulders. This is annoying, as well as frightening.

One conclusion is that the Waker is the ghost of a former patient, demanding the complete attention of his or her caregiver. But it is also possible that the presence is the shade of a nurse unfamiliar with the longer shift breaks, insisting that the staff return to work immediately.[10]

Other eerie happenings have occurred on Ward South 3. Registered nurse Sonia Lee was working in the very early hours of the morning at a time when the lights on the ward were turned down to permit the patients to sleep. As she busied herself near the nursing station, she happened to glance down the long, dimly lit corridor. Suddenly she was aware of a small light, "much like a candle flame," flitting along the far end of the hall beyond the last patient room.[11] The light's movements were quick and erratic, leaving no doubt that the source was not of this world. Sonia had no desire to venture down to the far end of the hall to investigate.

Friends and neighbours pose in front of the Mohr House, *c.* 1893.

CHAPTER SEVEN

MORE HAUNTED HOUSES

VERNON'S LITTLE GIRL GHOST

For well over a century the ghost of a child has been bound to the house where she lived in Vernon, British Columbia. Seven-year-old Louisa "Lonna" Mohr died under such tragic circumstances that her spirit has become earthbound.

When Charles Mohr, his wife, Elizabeth, and their family moved to Vernon in 1892, Lonna was the second-youngest of five children. In the newly incorporated city, Charles worked as a carpenter and lathe turner for the Smith and Clerin Sawmill, and his abilities as a carpenter enabled him to build two houses in the city. The home occupied by Mohr was on Pleasant Valley Road and was completed in 1893.

Charles Mohr was said to be a loving husband and father, and a popular member within his church and the community at large. He appeared to have settled comfortably into a quiet life in his new hometown. However, in the spring of 1894, a sad event befell the family. Lonna complained of a severe toothache, and according to local lore, the family sent for a doctor who lived in the much larger city of Kamloops, which then would have been a long trip by road. The physician, it is said, took a week to arrive by horse and buggy, and by then it was too late: Lonna had died of blood poisoning.

Historical evidence reveals a somewhat different story. In

1894, a rail service connected Vernon with Kamloops.[1] In the same year the city had three physicians, although no dentist had opened a practice there. Lonna was taken to a dentist in Kamloops where her sore tooth was extracted. Apparently, the procedure did not go well, and Lonna seems to have returned home in even more pain than she had suffered earlier. Dr. Osborne Morris of Vernon was sent for, but he could do nothing to save her life. Through the final week of March, her condition worsened, and at last, the child died of an acute infection on Saturday, March 31. Of young Lonna, the local newspaper stated that she "bore with extreme fortitude the extreme pain attendant upon her sickness."[2]

The next day, the funeral was held at the Mohr home and she was buried in what came to be known as the Old Vernon Cemetery. The sad story of the child's death would have ended at that point, had it not been that the graveyard was not properly maintained by the city and was regarded by the citizens as a disgrace. In 1901 a new cemetery was opened on Pleasant Valley Road, and a few years later Charles decided to move his daughter's remains to this more agreeable resting place. Given the pain Lonna had suffered following her visit to the dentist, her father was convinced that the man had botched the procedure. Her exhumation allowed Lonna's father to examine the body, and what he saw confirmed the terrible truth: a severe fracture to the child's jaw was evident. Half a century before the advent of antibiotics, the fractured jaw would have provided an ideal site for the growth of pathogens, and there would have been virtually no chance of the little girl's recovery.

Charles Mohr died on May 14, 1918, at age sixty-five. Soon after his death, Mohr House passed out of the Mohr family's possession.

By the 1940s, the house seems to have gained a reputation as being haunted. This unwelcome notoriety arose partially from the gothic appearance of the large dwelling, with its seven gables and mansard roof (where bats often lived). Yet as the years passed, more than just the aspect of the house prompted ghost stories. As often happens, most of these tales have been lost over time; however, there is a second-hand account of an Edmonton woman who lived in the house as a child.

One day the young girl was standing in a room on the main floor in front of a large window when an unseen hand pushed her away. The act saved her life, for a vehicle that was wildly out of control crashed through the wall, splintering the window where she had been standing. Although the story seems too incredible to be true, later events revealed that the ghost of Lonna is no weak presence: she has been capable of physically interacting with the material world.

By late in the twentieth century, the old dwelling had been divided into apartments. During this period, there was an abnormally high turnover of tenants, and it is not difficult to conclude why. About 2006, Gabriel Newman, who operates Ghost Tours of Vernon, was surprised to receive a phone call from across the Pacific. It was from a New Zealand woman who was seeking information about Mohr House. She had visited Canada more than a decade earlier and had spent a year in Vernon. Now, she had no contacts in the city, but she had searched the Internet, found Gabriel's website, taken a chance, and telephoned him. "To begin with," Gabriel recalled, "I didn't tell her anything about the house. She just called me, explained where she had lived in Vernon, and gave me infor-mation about her experiences in the house."[3] She finished by saying, "Do you know anything about this or did I go crazy?"[4]

She had lived in a suite in Mohr House during the year she and her partner spent in Vernon, and even years later, the strange occurrences during her short time there continued to bother her. Their introduction to the house was out of the ordinary, for as they arrived, the former tenant was leaving. They entered the suite and she saw that he had not taken a set of barbells. She opened the window and called out to him that he had forgotten his weights. "Just throw them down to me," he answered. "I'm not coming up!"

During their time in the apartment, Lonna made herself known. Many weird events occurred, including dishes moving on their own and then crashing to the floor. Once a teacup floated in midair, before falling.

Although Lonna did not seem to like the woman's partner, the atmosphere was not particularly negative—that is, until the day they began moving out. Ghosts clearly do not like change, and Lonna is no exception. On her way down the stairs, the departing tenant felt someone push her from behind. She had to grab onto the handrail to prevent a headlong fall to the bottom. Of course no one was behind her—no one visible at least.

Ironically, in 1996 Lonna, who had endured so much pain and possibly death as a result of a botched tooth extraction, was to have her one-time home turned into a dental office. A West Vancouver dentist, Dr. Karl Denk, purchased the house and restored its exterior. The main floor was converted into the offices of his new practice, the Pleasant Valley Dental Clinic. The apartments above the new business were modernized and rented.

At times, Lonna has been seen as a solid apparition. During the reconstruction of the building, workers sometimes noticed a little blond girl peeking out from behind a wall.[5] They wondered how a child could have made her way onto the closed work site.

Many of the weird events have occurred since the conversion

of the house. On occasion, the door to the dental offices would open slowly, but no one would be standing there. The electronics have been particularly affected by the ghostly presence: the television sometimes turns on and off for no logical reason, and the electrically controlled dental chairs, when not in use, have been seen to swivel on their own.

One day a young patient came in to have her teeth cleaned. The little girl had brought her teddy bear with her, but after the procedure, the plush toy could not be found. According to the receptionist, Carol Giesbrecht, "We looked high and low for this teddy bear. The little girl was so upset, she was crying."[6]

Before they left for the evening, the clinic staff asked the office cleaners to look out for the child's cherished possession. The next morning when Carol came to work, the teddy bear was sitting on the reception desk. She phoned the family, who quickly retrieved it. That evening when the cleaners came on duty, Carol thanked them for finding the teddy bear. They looked surprised and asked, "What teddy bear?"

One of the strangest events happened after closing time. Carol was completing her work at her desk when suddenly she felt a "wind" blow past her, "which was creepy." Not wanting to be alone, she got up to see if the dental assistant was still in the office. Carol recalled:

> Just then [the assistant] screamed in the back of the room. When I got to her, her purse was all over the floor and things had fallen out. I asked, "What happened?" And she said, "I don't know. It was the weirdest thing. It was like someone ran into me and knocked my purse off my shoulder." Just then we heard thump, thump, thump, up the back steps.

As they were getting ready to leave, both women felt another gust of wind, as though something had rushed past them. "As we looked through the glass doors we saw this little blond girl in full stride in the reflection of the glass doors running around the corner." It struck Carol that she was, like any child her age, simply playing. The spectre was wearing an old-fashioned black dress with a white collar. (This was likely the item of clothing in which she was buried.)

Lonna died in terrible pain, probably as a result of the gross incompetence of a dentist. Yet other children die under even more horrible circumstances, and their spirits do not remain earthbound. Why does the ghost of this unfortunate child remain to haunt Mohr House?

THE TERRIFYING WOMAN IN WHITE

The house at 2043 West Second Avenue in the Kitsilano district of Vancouver was like others on the block. In 1956, when George and Shirley Norris and their three children, Jackie, Robert, and Ken, moved in, there seemed nothing unusual about their new house. However, when George began major changes to the dwelling, the renovations unleashed an entity that was extremely frightening and even dangerous.

Typical of the architectural style of the turn of the twentieth century, the house had a partially sunken basement, a main floor with an entrance hall leading to the living room, a dining room, and a kitchen, which was at the rear. In the hall was the staircase leading to the second floor, which contained three bedrooms, a laundry room, and separate rooms for the toilet and bathtub. Another stairway led to a high attic that contained two more bedrooms.

The house, which was over fifty years old by the early 1960s, was in need of upgrading: it was not properly insulated, and the cold winter winds blew in from English Bay. About 1962, George replaced the old wooden siding with a stucco exterior that better kept out the cold drafts. At the same time he added a new front porch. After the work began, George and Shirley were aware that they were now living with a ghost.

Their first realization came when the lights in different rooms throughout the house would turn off or on by themselves—there did not seem to be a logical explanation. Areas of the house were on separate circuits, and if there was a problem, it should have been limited to only one electrical pathway.

The lights in the basement appeared to be the greatest problem. They would turn on at odd hours of the night. Ken and Robert were at first blamed for forgetting to switch them off, but it soon became obvious it was not their fault. George had installed an outside light over the basement door that was wired in series with the basement lights so that if anyone turned the lights in the basement on, that bulb would also be on.

Late one evening, after the family had retired, the household was awakened by a terrifically loud noise—it sounded as if someone had taken a jackhammer to the concrete floor in the basement. The cacophony brought everyone downstairs. When they peered out the kitchen window, they could see the lights from the basement illuminating the ground, but the bulb over the entrance was *off*. Because this light was wired in series, if the bulb had simply burned out, the basement lights would not have been on. George summoned the courage to go down to the basement. As he grasped the door handle, the noise stopped instantly and the light reflected in the backyard went out. When he entered the room and switched on the lights, nothing could be seen, nor was anything out of place.

Ordinary sounds penetrated several levels of the old house. When George was working in the basement, Ken could hear him in the attic. Thus it was no surprise that the rumble of the washer, or even footsteps crossing the linoleum floor of the laundry room, could be heard directly below in the kitchen. There were noises, though, that could not be explained.

A neighbour stopped by to speak with George one evening, and while he and Ken and their visitor were in the kitchen, the conversation was suddenly interrupted. "We heard a noise of something jump down from the ironing board and scamper across the floor," Ken recalled.[7] It sounded like the swift movements of a cat. Ken looked at his father and said, "We don't have any cats." His father looked back knowingly, and nodded. George did not go upstairs to investigate.

The entity intended to severely frighten the Norris family. One day, Shirley was visiting the neighbours, and Ken was alone in his room. As he played with a toy, he heard a voice calling "Kenny, Kenny, Kenny" from somewhere in the house. It sounded like his father, so Ken jumped up and ran down the stairs. The voice continued to call his name, and the sound was coming from the basement. "Just as I reached the basement door, I got a chill and my hair stood up on end." At that moment Ken remembered his father was at work. He never discovered what awaited him in the basement.

One night George was lying in bed when he turned on his side. To his surprise, in the doorway, his wife was beckoning him to join her in the hall. He sat up and was about to place his feet on the floor when he glanced toward the other side of the bed to discover Shirley asleep beside him. George slipped back under the covers, turned away from the door, and eventually fell asleep.

Shirley also had a strange experience one night. Jackie, who was much older than Robert or Ken, had her bedroom on the second floor. Through the night Shirley heard what she thought was her daughter moving quickly down the hall to the toilet. Moments later she heard what sounded like retching. In the morning she questioned Jackie about her visits to the toilet. Her daughter was surprised, telling her mother that she had enjoyed a good night's sleep.

One day when Ken was six, he climbed the stairs to the attic and opened his door. Standing before him was a woman wearing a white dress. She was bending forward as if looking at something, but where her eyes were fixed there was nothing to see. As he came into the room she raised her eyes and stared at the little boy. He had no doubt that she was a real person, for he turned and ran downstairs and asked his mother who the lady in his room was. Shirley went upstairs with her son, but no one was there.

Ken and Robert had bedrooms on opposite sides of the attic hallway, which created a problem. If Ken, who never closed his curtains, left his door open, the streetlight shone directly into Robert's room. One night Robert was awakened by what he thought was the glare of a streetlight in his eyes. He was about to go across the hall and shut his brother's door when the light began to take on a human form. As he watched in terror, it materialized into what appeared to be a woman wearing white. She walked into his room and sat on the end of his mattress—he could feel her weight depress the bedsprings. Frightened, he pulled the covers over his head. After what must have seemed like hours, the weight seemed to release. Eventually he peeked out from beneath the covers, but there was no one to be seen.

The stairway to the second floor had been built in a U-shape with a series of landings. One day Shirley was descending from the top when she felt a sudden pressure on her back. It exerted enough force to send her sprawling down the stairs. Fortunately there were only a few steps to the next landing and she was not seriously injured. However, it was obvious that the Woman in White was a dangerous entity.

In 1971, the house was sold to a property developer who planned to demolish it. In the interim the Norris family, who had moved nearby, still had possession, and one day Ken and two friends decided to play in his old home. As the three boys moved through the house, Ken went upstairs to the attic while his friends were in different areas. A feeling of fear, like nothing he had experienced before, suddenly swept over Ken. He ran down the stairs and out the front door where the other two boys immediately joined him. Each had experienced an overwhelming feeling of terror at the same moment, and Ken never returned to the house. Today, an apartment building stands in its place.

THE TRAVELLER

While ghosts are usually attached to one location, voyageurs have the ability to follow individuals from one place to another. At times they may follow a person home from work and remain there only a short time. In other instances, an entity might follow a person from one house to another over many years. As one Saskatchewan resident discovered, her ghost was able to travel many kilometres from its original haunt. This ghost certainly made its presence known, and its actions could chill her to the bone.

In 1969, shortly after Candis and Stan were married, they moved into a farmhouse near the little village of Mortlach, Saskatchewan, 115 kilometres west of Regina. The large, four-bedroom house was old and in need of repair, but for the young farm couple who were beginning with little money, it was at least affordable. It did not take Candis long to discover that there was something odd about their home.

Particularly when Stan was at his baseball club late at night and Candis was alone in the living room or the kitchen, she would hear doors slam upstairs, but she would convince herself that it was the result of drafts that were common in the old house. Sometimes she would wake up and see a "gelatinous sort of a figure" in the darkness, but she would decide that it was only her imagination.

Other unexplained episodes, though, simply seemed peculiar. Sometimes when Stan and Candis retired for the night and turned the thermostat down, they would discover in the morning that the furnace had been turned up. Similarly, windows that Candis knew had been closed at night would be open when she arose the next day. Since there were only two people living in the house, they could only blame each other, yet Candis knew that these incidents happened far too often to be explained as simple absentmindedness.

Common items around the house would frequently be missing. The master bedroom had a large double closet but oddly, rather than the round pole that is usually placed horizontally in a closet, this one had a bar with slots drilled along it where clothes hangers could be inserted. This system had its advantages, for it kept all the clothes on the hangers neatly separated. It limited the space available, but it did keep Stan's work clothes and dress wear apart—not that that was much of a problem. As Candis noted, "My husband was a farmer so he didn't have much need for many dress-up clothes. He had one pair of pants, two shirts, and one tie."[8]

One evening during the fall, as they were preparing to attend a wedding, Stan opened the closet to retrieve one of his two good shirts, but to his surprise the slot from which it usually hung held nothing. Frustrated, Candis and Stan searched for the missing item.

Stan chose his remaining shirt, but when he turned to the dresser to take out his tie, it was not in its usual place either. Stan was sure his wife had misplaced an important part of his wardrobe, but Candis believed he had somehow managed to leave his shirt and tie at his father's house. Because the wedding was in Moose Jaw where his father lived, Stan borrowed a tie and was able to attend the event properly attired.

The missing shirt and tie remained a mystery. Several months passed, and as Candis dressed for work one morning, she recalled, "I opened up the closet doors, and I just turned cold." All of the clothes had been placed in separate holes at one end of the closet. "Hanging in the centre was a hanger with the missing shirt on it, buttoned up to the top, and the tie neatly knotted under the collar." Not surprisingly she remembered, "I was totally freaked out." What was fascinating was that someone or something had deliberately arranged the closet to draw attention to Stan's missing shirt and tie. Candis's husband, a confirmed skeptic concerning ghosts, was nevertheless shocked.

Another occurrence was positively frightening. The windows in the master bedroom faced west, and during the warm prairie summers, the room became so hot it was impossible to sleep. Stan and Candis's solution was to move to the cooler north bedroom. This space was much smaller, and the pitch of the roof limited the headspace on one side of the room.

Strangely, although both were sound sleepers and the temperature in the north bedroom was certainly more comfortable, Candis and Stan had a great deal of trouble sleeping there. At the time, they did not think that their sleeping problems were the result of something unnatural—only later did they recall how the room affected them.

Several years after they married, Candis became pregnant with their first child. The couple decided to use the north bedroom as a nursery, choosing a lilac colour for the walls and painting the ceiling white. The access to the attic was also in the nursery, so the panel covering the ceiling opening received a fresh coat of white paint.

Like most mothers, Candis enjoyed readying the room for the baby. One day she took a load of newly washed clothes upstairs to fill the dresser drawers in the nursery, and when she pushed open the door to the room, she froze. The ceiling panel had been moved aside, revealing the gaping entrance to the attic. Yet that was not all that left her terrified. From the hole in the slanted ceiling, and down the wall, were handprints—the palm and fingers of each print was outlined in soot. The blackened trail looked as if someone had crawled along the ceiling and down the wall—something no human could do. She had been to the nursery shortly before the prints appeared, so she was aware that it had occurred very recently.

While the entity had undoubtedly been present in the house when she and Stan had arrived, it was not "housebound," as Candis was to discover. In the early 1970s, she and Stan, with their two daughters, left the old farm dwelling and moved into a two-storey duplex in Moose Jaw. Like the farmhouse, the new home had an attic access in the children's room. One day while she was at work, Candis received a call from her daycare saying that they needed diapers for one of her children so, taking her lunch break, she hurried home to pick up the supplies. As she entered the room, she was shocked. "The attic board was moved and the handprints were down the wall." They were the same kind of finger and palm prints that she had seen in the nursery in the Mortlach house almost fifty kilometres away.

The ghost accompanied Candis and Stan when they moved to another house in Moose Jaw. It was never seen but there was no doubt that it was still with the family, for objects continued to disappear at an alarming rate. For Candis, who is a very organized person, the ghost's behaviour was particularly frustrating. Household items she had tucked away would be missing from their proper place. For Stan, who denied the ghost's existence, the repeated disappearance of little day-to-day things he needed, such as combs and toothbrushes, was annoying.

One Sunday in December in the late 1970s, it was time to ready the house for Christmas. After bringing home the holiday tree, Candis and Stan went downstairs to take out the decorations. When they found the stand, a typical three-legged support with a centre hole for the tree, one piece was missing: only two of the three legs were in the box. The third leg was nowhere in the basement or the workroom. Much to the children's disappointment, the tree could not be decorated that night.

The next night, Stan had a meeting, but Candis was home and thought she would look again for the missing part of the stand. "I went downstairs and I walked into the workroom, and the Christmas tree stand was sitting on top of one of the boxes," Candis recalled. "The third leg, completely covered in dust, and with no fingerprints on it, was sitting there too."

Candis did not touch the piece and waited for Stan to come home. When he arrived about eleven o'clock, Candis asked, "Did you find the other leg to the Christmas tree stand?"

"No."

"Well I did," Candis said.

"Where was it?"

"Come and look and I'll show you."

The couple returned downstairs. There in the workroom was the stand with the three legs on top of its box. While the dust had been smudged on the other two, an unblemished coating remained on the third leg. Candis recalled, "That was when he admitted that he believed that something strange was going on."

After growing up with the ghost, the children accepted the constant movement of things around the house as nothing unusual. If something disappeared, it would later turn up somewhere that was entirely out of place. Gradually, though, as time passed, items disappeared less often, and the presence seemed to fade away.

THE GHOSTS ON "PLEASANT" STREET

Brenda McPhedran's new home in a quiet southeastern Saskatchewan community was a complete change from her former residence in one of Alberta's oil-driven boomtowns. Although the area was experiencing a boom of its own, it had not altered the character of the community: there was a feeling of permanency about the town—through good times and bad, it would last. Her home, built of bricks and mortar, was also a symbol of endurance. In its long history it had stood up against many prairie winters. What she did not expect was that in her house the past was all too real. It could reach out and touch her.

Shortly after moving in, she was aware that something strange was happening. Brenda's bedroom was on the lower level (the basement), and after retiring for the night she would be awakened about three o'clock in the morning by voices coming from above her head. "It sounded as if a movie was playing upstairs. I'd hear a man mumbling. I'd assume he was telling jokes, because then I'd hear a woman laugh."[9] At first Brenda thought that her television upstairs had turned on, but when she checked, the set was off and the room was dark. As it continued, she noticed that when she climbed the stairs, the sounds stopped.

During Brenda's years in the house, the man's voice followed by a woman's laughter has been repeated many times. Usually in the middle of the night, voices in conversations are also heard, but it is always impossible to distinguish what they are saying.

The ghost that haunts this Saskatchewan
house has become more active over time.
COURTESY OF DIANE BELYK

While such sounds are probably recordings from the past,
and therefore not conscious entities, there appears to be at least
one ghost actively haunting the house. Within the first few
months in her new home, Brenda had the impression that she
was being watched. "It was not a bad feeling," she said. It was
not malevolent but gave her the sense it was simply curious.
She was not alone in her feeling that the house has an unseen
occupant. Brenda's friend John visited from Vancouver Island,
and during his stay, he had the feeling that wherever he was on
the upper level, someone was following him. Finally he turned
toward his invisible stalker and said, "Leave me alone!" From
then on the feeling went away.

Brenda believes the ghost has become accustomed to her presence and is now more active. The sound of footsteps upstairs began to be heard in the early hours of the morning. At times, too, she hears footsteps on the stairway to the basement.

Recently, she was awakened by what sounded like marbles rolling across the floor above her head. There can be no reasonable explanation for the occurrence, for the floor is carpeted. Under the carpet, though, is a hardwood floor, where at one time a little boy could have played with the "aggies."

Initially, the ghost restricted its activities to the upper level. Lately, though, it has become bolder and ventured downstairs. "I've woken up some nights," Brenda said, "and I can feel a cold hand touching my arm. It's a weird feeling." Yet, even under these circumstances, it does not convey a sense of malevolence. "I wake up and I'm startled," she said, "but I never feel I have to turn on the light, and I can't sleep." Brenda believes it is simply inquisitive, and she is quite willing to share her old brick house on the pleasant street in that little prairie town.

TWO HAUNTS

The North Cariboo district of British Columbia, which includes Quesnel, Wells, and Barkerville, has a long haunted history. When Donna McArthur moved from Vancouver Island to her spouse's home on the outskirts of Quesnel in 1992, she was surprised at how calmly John regarded the ghostly presence that haunted the property. John had thought it unnecessary to mention that the house was haunted until Donna had her own experience with the ghost. One afternoon, soon after moving in, she was talking on the phone in the kitchen when she happened to look up and see the silhouette of a man pass by. "He had a cowboy hat on or a brimmed hat," Donna recalled. "He was solid black and quickly passed the window."[10] The figure walked with a purposeful gait, as though he were going somewhere. Shaken, Donna walked into the next room and told John what she had seen.

"Oh," he said, "I see him all the time. He goes across the deck about the same time almost every night."

Later, Donna was in another room when the family dog gave warning of their trespasser. Even when the silhouette had passed the deck, the dog seemed to follow something with its eyes, as if the ghost were walking away from the house down their long driveway.

Donna and John found some aerial photos of their property, and it was possible to make out the faint outline of a trail through their land. Could their "cowboy" visitor have been a reflection from the distant past, caught forever in a trek that took him over their deck? This seemed to be a logical conclusion for he was never seen in the house.

Although their relocation had nothing to do with their ghost, the couple did not remain in the first house long before they sold it and moved to a newer one on the north side of Quesnel. The house had been built in the 1980s on property that once held an older dwelling, dating to at least the 1950s. Although the house was not very old when Donna, John, and their family moved in, it had had a number of former residents. Donna was surprised that, according to neighbours, one set of tenants had lasted only a month before moving on, claiming that the house had ghosts. Had Donna, John, and the children left one haunted house only to move into another?

The answer was not long in coming. Soon after moving in, Donna was home alone working at the computer when she heard a loud creak as one of the doors farther down the hall swung closed. There was no doubt what the sound was, for she could hear the latch click into the striker plate. Wondering what had caused this, she got up and walked into the hallway. To her amazement, the doors all stood ajar. This was only the first of many eerie experiences.

Members of the family frequently heard loud thumps and bumps coming from unoccupied rooms, only to discover when they investigated that no damage had been done. Nor was anything ever out of place.

On many occasions, John, Donna, and the children saw a fleeting shadow figure that was less distinct than the cowboy ghost from their former house. At first, when Donna caught a glimpse of it, she thought the spectre was her fifteen-year-old son walking into the dining room. But when she looked up she was shocked. It moved along the hallway and entered the dining room before it suddenly dissolved. The shape was not much over one and a half metres tall and appeared partially transparent with a blurry outline. It could have been either male or female.

Not only family members saw the ghost. One day, Donna's friend Cathy stopped by. The two women were at the kitchen counter, looking at photos. Cathy was facing the opening to the dining room and Donna was opposite her. A strange expression crossed the visitor's face.

Surprised, Donna asked, "What's the matter? Don't you like the picture?"

"It's not that," Cathy said. "Something just walked into your dining room." She went on to explain that, before it suddenly disappeared in plain view, she saw a shadow move from the hallway to the dining room.

The shape appeared to obey the laws of physics, for light in the visible spectrum does not pass through an opaque object. Although the shape was not solid, it did screen the light. Several times, John has sat in the family room watching television when the light from the hallway has been temporarily blocked out, as though a figure has walked by in front of the doorway.

The shadow was not the only sighting. One night Donna was in bed watching television, "when just beyond the television in the corner a grey fuzzy ball dropped from the ceiling and went down the corner of the wall to the floor." Then it simply dissolved. Although she was the only witness to the event that night, later John saw a ball materialize on the ceiling near the door on the opposite side of the room. As in Donna's sighting, it also fell to the floor. While neither Donna nor John was aware of what the balls might be, some researchers believe that these orbs are spirits that do not or cannot take on human shape. There are a number of controversial photos that purport to show faces within these balls, but such images can be easily created today.

There was certainly no question that the entity desired to make itself known. When Donna's twenty-year-old son, Travis, visited from Vancouver Island, he was unaware that the house was the centre of paranormal activity. She had not felt it necessary to plant such a notion in his mind. However, following his arrival, Donna, who was at work, received a phone call from Travis. "Mom," he said, "this house is haunted!"

"Now, honey, why would you think that?" Donna said, with probably more innocence in her tone than she felt.

"Because," Travis answered, "I can hear someone walking in the hallway and your dog keeps going to go and see. And I keep getting up thinking someone just came home, and there's never anybody there."

John and Donna's daughter heard people talking in the dining room. The voices were only a murmur, and it was impossible to make out what was said, but she said that the speakers were women.

At times family members have heard their names called

when no one was in the vicinity. Although it is frequent during active hauntings, name calling tends to be very unnerving for the recipients. Donna and other members of her family experienced a cold sensation, together with a feeling that someone was standing behind them. When they turned around, there was no one there.

Like most presences that haunt old houses, the entity was not threatening. As in many such cases, the ghost seems to be demanding to be noticed. Donna and John find nothing scary about the occurrences at their house. "We like it here," Donna remarked, "and it makes it interesting. It takes away from the boring normal house where nothing happens."

Long-forgotten George Hirst, the first person buried in the Pleasant Street Cemetery,
received his memorial stone more than one hundred years after his death.
COURTESY OF DIANE BELYK

CHAPTER EIGHT

CEMETERY GHOSTS

THE MAN FORGOTTEN

Although much is made of haunted cemeteries, it is rare that entities remain in these cities of the dead. They are more likely to be found in or around the places where they lived or died, but they do sometimes remain at their graves. Several reasons have been suggested for this: they may be confused and do not know where to go, or the spirits may be angry about a wrong never redressed. It is also thought that they have been so forgotten that no one knows who is buried beneath an unmarked grave, and this indignity draws them to such a dreary place as a cemetery.

Given its population, the city of Kamloops, British Columbia, seems to have more than its share of very public ghosts.[1] The area around the Pleasant Street Cemetery is a centre of ghostly activity. Directly behind the burial site is the Sagebrush Theatre, which has been haunted for more than a generation by an entity popularly known as "Albert." Albert is a mischievous ghost who seems intent on playing tricks on members of the cast and crew.[2] In the 1970s, another mischievous ghost, whom they named "Herbie," bothered a couple living very near the cemetery. Herbie seemed to enjoy playing with electrical appliances. As often happens with playful ghosts, this couple became attached to Herbie and was sorry to leave him behind when they moved.

The best known of the cemetery hauntings is "the Man

Forgotten." When the Pleasant Street Cemetery opened, the first plot had no headstone. Moreover, on May 28, 1900, the name of the first man interred was not even written on the first line of the new burial registry.

George Hirst was born in England in 1865 and immigrated to Canada sometime before the turn of the twentieth century. Little is known about his life in Canada until the spring of the year 1900, when he was working as a watchman for the Canadian Pacific Railway (CPR) west of the Rockies. His job was to ensure that no sparks spread by passing railway engines burned the wooden bridges and trestles or set fire to the dry brush along the line.

While working in the vicinity of Notch Hill, eighty kilometres northeast of Kamloops, George was thrown off his horse and struck his head. He died on a train carrying him to Kamloops, but for some reason, no death certificate was ever issued and the accident escaped mention in the local press.

Following his burial, George's ghost was said to have wandered the Pleasant Street Cemetery, attempting to draw attention to his plight. The accounts of his activities, as often occurs in the oral tradition, have been lost over time, but the legend of the Man Forgotten and the haunting of the Pleasant Street Cemetery have persisted. Interestingly, over one hundred years after his death, George's great-granddaughter in England contacted the Kamloops Museum & Archives to find out where her ancestor was buried. (At the time of his death, the CPR would have notified his next of kin.) It was thus discovered that George Hirst's body was laid unrecorded in the first plot of the Pleasant Street Cemetery. George may now rest in peace, for a memorial stone marks his gravesite and a plaque marking the hundredth anniversary of the cemetery pays tribute to its first occupant.

Melissa Baker, museum educator at the Kamloops Museum & Archives, stands in front of the grave markers in the haunted Pleasant Street Cemetery.

COURTESY OF DIANE BELYK

Alexander Beale's grave marker tells its own story of a man unable to rest in peace.

Kamloops Museum & Archives educator Melissa Baker, who grew up in Kamloops, recalls that the cemetery was always a spooky place. It was not far from a high school, and its paths were shortcuts to the city. In the autumn, particularly when the wind blows through the trees and the branches creak and crack, it is not a place to linger. According to Melissa, who led the Kamloops Cemetery and Halloween Tours sponsored by the museum and archives, it was not unusual for weird things to happen during her stop at the Pleasant Street site. In the middle of one of her tours, the lights on the high lamp standards abruptly went out, and the plunge into darkness was frightening. On another tour, Melissa recalled, "I'd just explained that there are a lot of children buried here, when all these children, somewhere in the distance, started screaming. It was like they weren't there and all of a sudden they were there screaming. It was bizarre."[3] One can only imagine the effect on the tour group.

Though George Hirst has been laid to rest, strange things continue to happen at the Pleasant Street Cemetery.

THE LEGEND OF ALEXANDER BEALE

In 1907, Alexander William George Beale, aged twenty-seven, of Gloucester, England, moved to Canada and homesteaded near the small community of Drinkwater, twenty-nine kilometres southeast of Moose Jaw, Saskatchewan. During the three years he lived in the area, he was well liked and known for his generosity.

When an American, Frank Miller, who had come to town in early June of 1910, asked to borrow Alex's buggy, the farmer willingly obliged him. Unlike other residents of this pioneer community, Miller was untrustworthy. He overturned and wrecked the buggy and, not even bothering to tell the owner, rode the horse into town.

On Sunday, June 12, Alexander's buggy still had not been returned, so he rode into Drinkwater to confront Miller. Their dispute came to blows, and Miller, who had been in the wrong, received the worst of the fight; he swore to take revenge on the homesteader. Alexander then took his horse back to his farm. Some time after he rode for home, the townspeople noted that the American had also left Drinkwater.

Between ten and eleven o'clock that night, gunshots broke the stillness around the Beale farm. Alexander was found in the doorway of his house the next day, his body riddled with bullets. His horse was missing, and the obvious suspect, Frank Miller, could not be found. Believing the fugitive was on his way to the Montana Badlands, the local police used an automobile in an attempt to catch him before he crossed the border, but he escaped and was never heard of again.

Alexander Beale was buried in the Moose Jaw cemetery, and his plot remained unmarked for several years. Eventually his brother arrived from England and commissioned a monument. Since then a mystery has hung over the granite headstone.

In the early years, Moose Jaw residents took pride in their cemetery and vandalism was practically non-existent. Yet unlike other similar grave markers, Beale's obelisk-style monument was frequently found lying on its side. Although it was returned to its pedestal, it seemingly refused to remain upright. It began to crack so that it was no longer possible to place it back in its vertical position, and today it has been reduced to a pile of stones. The unexplained behaviour of the marker, some Moose Jaw residents believed, was the result of Alexander Beale's spirit remaining angry that his murderer had escaped justice.

THE STRANGE CASE OF THE TABOR LIGHT

On six continents, stories of ghostly lights flickering or gleaming mysteriously over marshy lowlands have been told and retold over the centuries. Every language has a different name for them—in England they are called will-o'-the-wisps. There, lore has it that the lights appear to lure unwary night travellers off the narrow paths, where they are then drawn below the surface of the bog. Near one remote location in Saskatchewan, these lights have also made their ghostly presence known and have in the past frightened many an unwary late traveller.

The origin of the Tabor Cemetery is unclear, but after the coming of the railroad in 1885, immigrants from Central Europe settled in what was then the Northwest Territories. Many of those early immigrant communities did not survive, and all that remains today to mark their place are a few isolated, weather-beaten gravestones.

In the first decade of the twentieth century, a number of Hungarian immigrants settled around what became the little hamlet of Yarbo, in southeastern Saskatchewan. Because of the language barrier, many of the older people remained isolated and did not quickly integrate within the broader Canadian culture. In the very early years, these immigrants looked upon the abandoned cemeteries with suspicion; for instance, they viewed with misgiving a little graveyard set back from a country road two-and-a-half kilometres from Yarbo, for, unlike their traditional cemeteries, it was not attached to a church.

Many farmers living around the Tabor Cemetery had seen a strange light over the marshland near the burial ground that then passed above the grave markers before disappearing. The Tabor Ghost Light, as the glowing orb came to be known, appeared frequently during the first years of the twentieth century, and then was not seen regularly again until 1913 when, it was claimed, a young suicide victim was buried in the graveyard. It was twenty-five years before the light again appeared regularly.

Although in the first years, the sightings of the Tabor Ghost Light were confined to the community of Yarbo, in the early winter of 1938, stories of the light became the topic of conversation in the much larger community of Esterhazy, twelve kilometres away. The incident that surprised Esterhazy took place on the Yarbo–Churchbridge road near the old cemetery. A Royal Canadian Mounted Police officer who was responsible for the district of Esterhazy was patrolling near the graveyard when he saw a light approaching his vehicle. At first he thought that it was a car or truck with one headlight out. He was about to pull the driver over, but, as it came closer to the police car, it became obvious that the light was not from a vehicle at all. The light seemed to skip along the surface of the road and then, to his amazement, bounce past his patrol car and veer into the ditch along the roadside. That the light had been seen by a police officer added credibility to the account.

About the same time, a young woman had an encounter with the light near the same place. After attending a bridge game at a neighbour's house, she was walking home along the Yarbo-Churchbridge road past the Tabor Cemetery. Stars glittered brightly overhead, and as she walked, she happened to glance around to see a light skipping along the road some distance behind her. Whether or not she had heard stories of the Tabor Ghost Light was never reported, but the behaviour of the glowing ball filled her with fear. She began to jog but discovered the eerie stalker was keeping pace with her. At last at a full run she reached her farmhouse, and only when she was able to close the door did she escape her ghostly pursuer.

When stories of the eerie light circulated in Esterhazy, citizens were divided about the validity of the accounts. For the community's better-educated residents, the notion of a ghost light seemed ridiculous. Others, however, were more open to the idea. But there was also an undercurrent of fear that swept through the town. Some residents claimed that a cemetery ghost light was a harbinger of doom, and, after its appearance, sudden deaths would soon follow. Bizarre crab-like creatures that were intended to be the Tabor Ghost Light were drawn on letters addressed to branches of the provincial government.

On Wednesday, November 23, 1938, twenty people gathered at the old cemetery. The majority of men and women who had driven from Esterhazy were skeptics, and undoubtedly their intention was to put an end to the "nonsense" of the Tabor Ghost Light stories. Their vigil, though, did not proceed as most of the group expected. On that night, before the astonished onlookers, the fast-moving light flitted and bounced over the frozen ground four separate times. The disbelievers were bewildered.

In Esterhazy, word of the sightings quickly spread, and more residents planned to visit the Tabor Cemetery. On Tuesday, November 29, a group that included some of the people who had witnessed the light the previous week, as well as more of Esterhazy's skeptics, prepared for an overnight vigil. The watchers, dressed in heavy coats, fur-lined hats, and warm mittens, waited seemingly in vain for the reappearance of the ghost light.

"I don't believe anyone has ever seen a light, and there is no such thing in this district. It is all imagination," one man said.

He had hardly uttered the words when another watcher, who had seen it a week earlier, shouted, "There it is again."[4]

The sighting had a profound effect on the witness. "Anybody telling [the former doubter] there is no such thing as a light," wrote one reporter, "will receive a true story in reply about having seen the 'ghost' of someone buried in Tabor's cemetery who is not resting in his grave."[5]

On December 2, 1938, an Esterhazy pharmacist, E.B. Walker, his wife, and three others witnessed a light. Walker, from a site about three kilometres south of the cemetery, viewed it with binoculars and was able to provide an account of it. It was described as about the size of a nine-and-a-half-litre pail, and it appeared to burn like kerosene (blue). Yet it did not seem to illuminate the ground around it. The flame dimmed and brightened for up to two minutes before disappearing, only to reappear about forty-five metres from the last sighting. From two vantage points, the group observed the light for more than ten minutes.

Walker's report differed from most others, for the light was usually described as moving rapidly and its colour varied between pink and red. Moreover Walker was some distance away. The orb was frequently seen at the southern edge of the cemetery and it would then move up the brow of the hill to the north side.

Chemical explanations for the light generally related to the existence of swamp gas (hydrocarbons)—the combustible component being methane. While it is true that methane, under the right conditions, will ignite when exposed to the atmosphere, it burns with a bluish or greenish light, not reddish or pinkish as described by most eyewitnesses.

Some residents living not far from the turn-off to the graveyard wrote the Regina *Leader-Post* to tell of "bumping over the rutty, frozen cemetery road at sixty miles an hour in an effort to track down the light, but it always stays the same distance ahead of them."[6]

At the height of the furor, armed men carrying shotguns patrolled the area around the cemetery. One farmer even unloaded a barrel of lead pellets at it.

Between November 7 and December 2, 1938, probably more than three dozen people, on many different occasions, saw the light. With interest mounting, more and more people were crowding into the cemetery, and near the end of the first week of

December, authorities, fearing damage to the tombstones, barred the gate. With no access to the burial ground, the story of the Tabor Ghost Light disappeared from the province's press, and interest in the phenomenon faded completely.

It seems unfortunate that the accounts from the witnesses to the event were never collected in an archive and have been lost; thus, it is necessary to rely on press coverage. There were two different types of lights: the first was the "darting light" that was seen near the cemetery, and the second was stationary and was seen in a boggy area several kilometres from the burial ground.

One of the most interesting stories about the second type of light appeared in the press fourteen years afterward. John Bubnick, administrator for the village of Esterhazy, began to farm the land across the road from the Tabor Cemetery. One summer evening John was driving his team across the fields toward his farmhouse. The sun had long set and the last glow of twilight was fast fading behind the gently rising hills to the west.

As he urged his horses on, he saw the glow of what he thought was a gasoline lantern in the distance. John's father worked the adjoining farm, and John believed it must be his wife returning home from her in-laws' house. The light was not moving, and he wondered if she had dropped something in the field and was searching for it. He turned his team in that direction and when he approached the light, he stopped suddenly. The orb hovered about a metre above the ground, and it was extremely bright—so bright that he could see the brass buckles on the horses' harness shine in its glow.

John called to his wife, but no voice broke the stillness. Puzzled, he stepped down from the wagon and took a few steps toward the light, and it simply disappeared. When he reached home his spouse was waiting for him. The next day, when John searched the area, there was no clue of what had produced the light.

The light was unusual, for instead of darting quickly just above the ground, the orb hovered in one spot for some time— long enough for John to approach quite close. Yet he did not have the time to take the few extra steps necessary to see it clearly. Possibly its sudden disappearance was a coincidence, but it vanished almost at the moment when John might have discovered what it was.

The lights witnessed by John Bubnick, and John Walker and his companions, appear to belong to a class by themselves, for they remained almost motionless. Also the colour of the flame in both cases was toward the blue spectrum, indicating methane.

Although what Walker and his companions observed could have been swamp gas, the sightings took place at the beginning of a cold prairie winter, when methane would not easily have broken through the surface of the frozen bog. The idea that swamp gas was responsible for the majority of the 1938 cemetery sightings is simply not plausible.

Even in the realm of the paranormal, the Tabor Ghost Light is a conundrum. One can do no better than quote Winston Churchill: "It is a riddle, wrapped in a mystery, inside an enigma."[7]

CHAPTER NINE

VISITATIONS

THE MORNING VISIT

When Daniel was in his late teens, he was a problem for his stepmother, Maureen Clayton. The lure of a full-time job and earning "big money" was a powerful inducement to him to leave high school. Well aware of the long-term consequences of failing to graduate, both she and his father, Ron, strongly opposed Daniel's plans to drop out of school, but because Maureen was not his biological mother, the youth resented her interference. Tensions ran high.

One morning, probably about eleven o'clock, Maureen was busy in her kitchen; after another argument over school, angry thoughts about her stepson were passing through her mind. As she bent forward to close the dishwasher, she was aware of a man standing less than two metres away. The solid apparition was so real that he could easily have been mistaken for a living person, but it would have been impossible for anyone to enter the kitchen without her knowledge. Maureen froze and her hair stood on end.

He was an imposing figure in his early sixties, tall and broad-shouldered, with reddish brown hair liberally sprinkled with grey. He was wearing blue denim overalls and was clean-shaven, but had a somewhat unkempt look that suggested a person who toiled long hours in a physically demanding job.

Although he said nothing audible, she received his words telepathically. *Don't be thinking that about Daniel*, he communicated. Instantly the image disappeared. Moments later, Ron entered the kitchen and Maureen told him about her experience.

Ron had no idea who the visitor could have been, as he did not seem to resemble anyone in Daniel's family. However, there may be a clue in his dress. Blue denim bib overalls have long been the uniform of the farmer, and the apparition in the kitchen may have been an ancestor from many generations ago who came back to protect Daniel from Maureen's demands. Coming as the visitor did from another time, he was blind to the realities of the twenty-first century. Daniel did go on to finish high school and, as he matured, his perspective of the world changed. At the time, the visitor gave Maureen the idea that Daniel's adolescent years were a difficult period, and they would not last forever. The morning visit was something that she will never forget.

THE ROAD BACK

Something was wrong. The feeling was not one of the fleeting concerns people experience when family members are away from home. This was profound. As Jean Manifold stood in the lineup at the Vernon, British Columbia, supermarket on that August afternoon in 1990, she suddenly knew something terrible had happened.

On the way home, Jean faced the panic welling up within her. Her children had gone on a trip with their father to the United States, and Jean was concerned that they had been in an accident. When she phoned the Royal Canadian Mounted Police, the clerk told her that no serious mishaps had been reported on the route they were taking. Although the information should have been reassuring, the dreadful gnawing feeling in the pit of her stomach did not decrease.

As the hot afternoon passed into the warm evening, Jean continued to worry. At about seven o'clock, the telephone rang—it was her mother, calling to say that Jean's father, Sam, who also lived in Vernon, had not returned home. He was an amateur prospector, and it was not unusual that he was away from home for several days at a time, but he had always let his family know where he was going and when he would return.

Well aware of the terrible premonition that had overwhelmed her that afternoon, Jean could not help but fear the worst. Two of her brothers drove into the backcountry and the next day, they found Sam's body at the bottom of a steep draw. He had died of a heart attack and probably tumbled to the bottom of the ravine.

The sudden death of Jean's father devastated her entire family. Her niece, Kristy, who worked in an Asian restaurant in the nearby city of Kelowna, told her employers about the distressing event, and they mentioned a ritual often performed in their region of China. On the seventh night after the passing of a family member, the loved one may return home to make a final visit. To reveal the road back, it is necessary to place a lighted candle beside a picture of the deceased. Then, to know they have returned, a feather pillow is placed at the head of the bed and pressed so it is firm enough to reveal the shape of the person's head. Finally, to expose any footprints, talcum powder is dusted on the floor leading from the door to the bed. Although the ritual sounded strange to Jean, she was willing to follow the simple instructions. Her mother, too, was skeptical, but willing to see what would happen.

About nine o'clock on the seventh evening after her father's death, Jean arrived at her childhood home. After her mother had retired for the night, Jean prepared the living room and bedroom according to the ritual. Then, after locking the front and back doors, she made herself comfortable on the couch—the same couch, she recalled, where her father had taken naps. Except for the soft glow cast by the candle, the living room was dark.

As she lay there, she heard every creak and groan of the house. Jean was finally drifting off to sleep when she was abruptly awakened by a familiar sound—it was the front door opening, the door she knew she had locked. At that moment she was frightened. Seconds later, she heard the distinctive sound of the latch clicking shut, and then her father was on his knees beside her. He was much younger—no grey streaked his dark hair. The fear that seconds earlier had been so overwhelming was gone, for she knew her dad would never do anything to hurt her.

As he looked at Jean he said, "If you had one good thing to say about me, what would it be?"

"Dad," she said, "you used to rub my legs whenever they were sore."[1] (Like many young people she had suffered from growing pains.)

Jean was about to continue when her father looked at the table with the candle and the picture. In the next moment he was gone.

As Jean recalled, a slight indentation could be seen in the pillow, and the talcum powder was to some extent disturbed, but such proof was unnecessary. He had taken that unknown road home to see her for the last time, and the couch where he appeared to her that night has always had a special place in her heart.

UNDER THE CHERRY TREE

Some individuals find that it is not people but places that are important. For someone who has created his or her own special place, it can be a vital last stop on earth.

When Judy and Clyde Douglas moved in next door, their elderly neighbour, Bill, dropped by and introduced himself. His family had grown up and moved away, and now he devoted most of his time to his garden. He loved the hours he spent tending his flowers and vegetables. The work was not easy for the small, stoop-shouldered man, but the property, near the corner of Eleventh Street and Kings Avenue in West Vancouver, was the envy of the neighbourhood.

Bill had a great sense of humour. He had a magnificent cherry tree that extended over the young couple's backyard, and when the fruit was ripe he and Judy would joke about the ownership of those branches.

In 1978, Judy returned from the hospital with their first child. She and Clyde had not seen Bill in his garden lately, but like most young couples, their world then centred on their newborn son, Ryan. One moonlit night, Judy had finished nursing the baby when she happened to look out the back window. To her amazement, Bill was standing under the cherry tree, wearing the old hat, pants, and plaid shirt that were his gardening clothes. Although she watched him for some minutes, he did not look up or acknowledge her. Judy wondered why he was up late at night in his backyard, and even stranger, in his gardening clothes.

The next day, Judy could hear people talking in Bill's backyard and from her window, she recognized them as his family. She went next door and found the elderly man's son, who told her that his father had died during the night. When she revealed what she had seen, he said that it would have been impossible for Bill to move from his bed, let alone to have dressed and stood in his backyard. When Judy thought about it later, it seemed as if Bill's spirit wanted to stop by and make one last visit to his beloved garden.

CHAPTER TEN

OTHER HAUNTS

THE HAUNTED REFORMATORY

Elaine was loved by the boys who had been sentenced to the Nisbet Youth Centre in Prince Albert, Saskatchewan, and she loved the young people who were housed in the locked facility. In fact, the boys meant so much to her that she did not want to leave them—even in death.

When Patricia Melsted-Chabot began work in the kitchen of the Nisbet institution, Elaine was the senior cook. She was a thin, short woman with dark hair, in her early fifties, who habitually wore dark clothing. Although she was not always on the best of terms with her fellow employees, she doted on the boys, who were mostly from First Nations families.

As in all such institutions, the kitchen in the Nisbet Youth Centre was a secure area because of the ready access to knives, but a number of trusted boys were either assigned general kitchen duty or enrolled in a cooking course. When Elaine was working, the young people looked forward to kitchen assignment, for she would give them special treats such as ice cream. She was someone who would listen to their problems.

Elaine was passionate about animals and lived alone in a trailer on a farm about fifty kilometres outside Prince Albert, where she cared for more than a dozen dogs and cats. With the exception of her boys at the centre, she had little else in her life.

Although Patricia and Elaine did not work together very long, they became friends.

Elaine's health was not good. She had worked more than twenty years for the government and was eligible for extended sick benefits, but she was reluctant to leave her boys.

In 2003, with Patricia's encouragement, Elaine finally left her job, and on November 24, she passed away peacefully. For Patricia, her friend's sudden death was a shock. At her funeral, many of Elaine's boys, now men filling responsible jobs in the community, crowded the pews. Sadly, in life she never knew the effect she had on so many of the youths who had once been in the Nisbet Centre.

One afternoon in early 2004, the lunch meal cleanup was finished and the boys had been sent from the kitchen. Patricia was at work at the grill preparing dinner, while her supervisor, Diane, was sitting at her desk nearby. Suddenly she turned to Patricia and demanded, "Lock those doors."[1]

"They are locked," Patricia answered.

Diane stood up from her desk and walked into the area where Patricia was working. "No," she said. "One of the boys just walked past you and through those doors."

Patricia could not believe what Diane had said. "There are no boys in here," she told her supervisor.

"A boy just walked from the cooler out these doors," Diane insisted. She went over to the doors and pushed against them. They were firmly locked. She turned back to Patricia and said, "Did you see anything?"

"No, I didn't see a thing," Patricia replied.

Diane was obviously shocked. "She just went pale," Patricia later recalled.[2]

On April 21, 2004, the Nisbet Youth Centre closed its doors and the boys were moved to an expanded facility in the city.

The new kitchen was not finished, so meals would continue to be prepared in the Nisbet Centre's kitchen and transported by van to the new dining room. Patricia and the other cooks were now working in a building with no residents. Without the need for stringent security there did not seem to be any need to lock the outside gate. However, because she worked the late shift, Patricia was alone in the unlocked building for several hours in the evening. Her last task was to fill out the paperwork required by her department.

One shift, Patricia finished mopping the kitchen floor and, because it was a warm evening, she left the outside door open so the tiles would dry quickly. Then she sat down at Diane's desk to begin the paperwork. As she filled out the reports, she became aware that she was not alone. "[I] saw someone walk from the cooler to the dining room through the [dining room] doors. I leaped to my feet thinking one of the boys had hidden in the cooler." Patricia opened the dining room doors and looked into an empty room. There was no one there. It was impossible for anyone to exit the other end of the long room in the time it took her to reach the doors. When Patricia turned around she began to shiver; the temperature in the kitchen had dropped drastically. Soon after this incident the new kitchen opened, and the old kitchen in the Nisbet Youth Centre was closed.

Later, it occurred to Patricia that neither she nor Diane had seen a boy, but the spectre of Elaine. She was a small, thin woman who wore dark clothing and could easily have been mistaken for one of the residents.

Elaine's death had come shortly before the closing of her long-time workplace. She loved the boys, and the shutting of the centre meant that the empty facility would have been, for one ghost, a very lonely haunt.

THE OLD MAN'S HOUSE

In the late 1980s, when Lynda Wood and her partner, Denny, moved into a house in an undeveloped part of Surrey, British Columbia, their quiet, dead-end road stood out in stark contrast to the subdivisions and strip malls that dominated much of Vancouver's largest suburb. Only two other houses occupied the block: one was across the road from where Lynda and Denny lived, and an elderly man owned the other house, which was on the same side of the road. Lynda recalled that the old fellow was short and thin, and habitually wore flannel, lumberjack-style shirts, winter or summer.

The old man had no visitors, nor did he even acknowledge the two neighbours who shared his block. Occasionally, he was seen in his yard, and it was said that he sometimes ventured down into the ravine behind his house. However, Lynda and Denny most often saw him walking along the highway leading to the city of Langley. Lynda thought it was surprising that the man, who looked to be well into his eighties and walked with a cane, was able to make such a long return trek.

Although the old fellow was less than friendly, Lynda tried to watch out for him because given his advanced age and reclusive behaviour, she could imagine that if he were ill or injured, he could remain in his house for days or even weeks without anyone being aware of his plight. As the months passed, though, the couple continued to see him on his regular walks along the highway.

One afternoon, Lynda and her friend Dianne had planned a shopping trip to one of the Surrey malls. Before leaving, Lynda decided to have a quick shower while Dianne waited in the dining room. Lynda had not long felt the flow of warm water over her body when there was a knock on the bathroom door, and Dianne called out over the sound of the spray that a fire truck and several police cars had gone down to the old man's house. She wondered if he was all right. Lynda turned off the shower and opened the window that faced his house.

As her friend had said, there was much commotion at the end of the block. Emergency vehicles with their lights on were at the house. However, Lynda could see the old man standing near his front door facing her—his back to the police and firemen as they came and went. He was wearing the yellow-and-black-checked shirt he often had on during his walks. As he watched the uniformed men and women pass by, he appeared angry. It must have been a false alarm, Lynda thought.

She towelled off and said to Dianne, "He's okay, but he looks very annoyed."[3]

A few minutes later, Lynda was dressing when Dianne called out that now an ambulance had pulled up to the house. Lynda looked out the window where she had a clear view. The old man was still standing beside his door facing in Lynda's direction, but now he looked even more upset, waving his cane back and forth in the air as if he were enraged.

Lynda wondered what had happened. As soon as she had dressed, the two women left the house, but as they walked down the stairs, a police car pulled into the driveway and an officer got out. "When was the last time you saw the fellow who lives at the end of the road?"

Lynda was about to say "A few minutes ago," when something stopped her. "Last Friday," she answered instead. "Is anything wrong?"

"He's dead," replied the officer.

The night before, the old man had been murdered in the course of a home invasion. Charges were never laid, but the police believed that the perpetrators were likely young people who thought that the old man had hidden a large sum of money in the house. Floorboards had been ripped up in search of the supposed hiding place. Only when Lynda and her friend had a chance to discuss what had happened did they realize that Lynda had not seen the victim; she had witnessed the ghost of the old man angrily shaking his cane at the fate that had befallen him.

TURNEY'S GHOST

Forestburg is a small community of fewer than nine hundred people, 175 kilometres southeast of Edmonton. For many years, coal mining has been an important part of the economy. Most residents today do not know that Forestburg was the site of a ghostly happening. A local mine owner, James Robert Turney, died on October 20, 1917. Turney seems to have been a very angry ghost who one day decided to show up at the mine. Digging out coal is dangerous work, and miners tend to be a superstitious lot; it was not surprising that, when Turney's ghost paid them a visit, the miners were not pleased to see him.

The first indication that something in the mine was amiss was strange noises. At first the miners blamed the noises on a workmate, but he was exonerated when the ghost of their former employer moved out of the shadow of the dimly lit tunnel. As they turned toward him, a fearful silence seemed to deaden the air. Those who knew Turney had no doubt that it was the former mine owner, and they ran in panic—all except one brave soul who threw a pick at the apparition. Once it struck Turney's ghost, the spectre vanished.

The miners went to visit the owner's wife, who lived in one of the finest houses in the district. She could offer no advice on "laying" the ghost; indeed she said the angry spirit had appeared many times to her. Once, she claimed, it had materialized carrying an axe and had chased her from room to room about the house.

Not only the miners and the widow witnessed the angry apparition. About midnight one night, the local liveryman was taking a passenger on the road that ran near the Turney Mine when they saw a figure standing still at the top of the derrick. Although it was impossible to identify the figure, there seemed little doubt that it was Turney, silhouetted against the moon.

When the newspapers picked up the story in 1922, no miner had gone near the pit for over a year, and without pumps operating continuously, the mine had flooded. The Turney residence, once one of the best houses in the area, was now deserted, and fell into ruin after his widow moved to British Columbia. If it had been Turney's ghost's intention to destroy all that he had built during his lifetime, he succeeded admirably.

OUR GHOSTLY ENCOUNTER

As a collector of ghost stories, and not a ghost hunter, I rarely come face to face with the subject of my books. The following event involved mainly my wife, Diane, who is my photographer, co-researcher, and travelling companion.

While I regard myself as open-minded regarding paranormal activity in general, Diane has been skeptical. Now, after an eerie night thrust her into one of the stories we were covering, she is no longer as unconvinced about preternatural occurrences. When we visited L'Auberge Clémence Bed and Breakfast, Diane met the ghostly nun who haunts the King Room.

To write true ghost stories, it is much better, whenever possible, to interview the witnesses in person rather than to rely on communications by telephone or email. For that reason, Diane and I decided to visit the Western provinces and interview as many people as possible. We left Vancouver on June 24, 2011, and arrived on July 14 at L'Auberge Clémence in Elie, Manitoba, some 2,250 kilometres distant. Along the way, we made many side trips in British Columbia and the Prairie provinces, and spoke with dozens of interesting people about their ghost experiences. (For more stories not in this book, visit Haunts West [www.hauntswest.com]).

We had planned to spend two nights at L'Auberge Clémence to rest before our drive back to the West Coast. It was a good choice for a stopover, because Jean and Linda Aquin, the owners of the bed and breakfast, have restored the former convent and created a beautifully landscaped garden. After speaking with Jean and Linda, we decided to stay in the King Room on the third floor, which was said to be haunted by the ghost of one of the sisters of St. Martha's Convent. (Even when the door to the room has been latched and locked, witnesses have seen it open on its own.)

The first night was not uneventful. In the morning we discovered that our locked door was ajar. On the second night, we interviewed Jean concerning the occurrences at their haunted bed and breakfast and did not go upstairs to our room until about 1:00 AM.

While I was in the bathroom, Diane slipped into bed. She was lying on her left side with her head on the pillow when she became aware that she could feel a weight, as if someone were lying beside her. The pressure had pulled on the sheet and bedspread that covered her. Her first thought was that I had returned, but that made no sense, for she would have heard movement in the room. She turned quickly to her right, but nothing was there. Thinking that it must have been her imagination, she adjusted the covers and turned back onto her left side. Scarcely had she rolled over than she felt the weight on the bed again. By now she thought this was really bizarre. Diane turned on her back and closed her eyes. Seconds later she felt a weight pressing on the mattress, but when she looked again nothing was visible.

At this time I returned to the bedroom. For Diane the "body" lying on the bed next to her was beyond anything she could readily accept, and for this reason she convinced herself that it was nothing more than her imagination. I would probably never have heard the story if this incident was all that occurred that night.

Later, Diane awoke and looked at the digital clock that read 2:50 AM. Suddenly, she heard a voice say, "Get up! Get up! Get up!" She described it as "sharp," "high-pitched," and "demanding." "The voice was in my right ear," she said.

Diane was wide awake, but she thought there must be a logical explanation for what had occurred. She later recalled, "At first I thought Linda was calling loudly to Jean, but when I realized it was almost three o'clock in the morning I knew it shouldn't have been happening, and it unnerved me." Fearing there might be a problem in the house, she got up and walked down the staircase as far as the second-floor landing, but there was not a sound coming from anywhere. Frightened, she locked the bedroom door and returned to bed. Eventually she fell asleep. In the morning, the door to our room was again ajar.

The spirit of the sister appears to have taken a special interest in us, particularly Diane. It is impossible for me to speculate why. I can attest that my wife does not have an overactive imagination. Never before or since has she heard a disembodied voice. For Diane, who had been skeptical about the existence of ghosts, her experience at L'Auberge Clémence has raised many difficult questions.

Introduction: On Ghosts and Hauntings

1   Quoted in Stuart Eskenazi, "Ghost Stories Haunt Pike Place Market," *Seattle Times*, June 25, 2007, accessed January 3, 2014, http://seattletimes.com/html/localnews/2003761417_mymarketghost25m.html.

2   There are many versions of this legend. It was alleged at the time that the girl turned to leave and fell down the stairs, but since a similar "accident" befell another daughter in his presence, this time on the third floor landing, the colonel seems to have a penchant for launching his children over the balustrade.

3   Cited in Daniel Cohen, *Encyclopedia of Ghosts*, 190.

4   In 2002, I and four other people did not see my late father-in-law, but heard his distinctive footsteps coming up the back stairs of his house. For the full account of this story, see the afterword in my book *Ghosts: More Eerie Encounters*, 211–214.

5   At one time Persinger's work was cited by skeptics to prove ghosts were nothing more than hallucinations created by individuals predisposed to right temporal lobe epilepsy, but rather than simply distinguishing this region of the brain as the creator of such experiences, the neuroscientist has identified it as a receiver of telepathic communication.

Chapter One: Haunted Attractions

1   Jay Russell, cited in Jeff Belanger, in *The World's Most Haunted Places: From the Secret Files of Ghostvillage.com*, 130–31.

2   *Lethbridge Herald*, April 19, 1992.

3   Personal interview with Diana Segboer, July 1, 2011.

4   *Macleod Gazette*, April 12, 1992.

5   *Lethbridge Herald*, April 19, 1992.

6   Segboer.

7   Telephone interview with Joyce Bonertz, August 11, 2011.

8   Segboer.

9   Bonertz.

10 Although it is not known whether Ed had a taste for cigars, given the times and his cowboy garb, he may have smoked cheroots.

11 Telephone interview with Lisa Regan, October 21, 2011.

12 Telephone interview with Andy Jenkins, August 23, 2011.

13 Telephone interview with Terry Daniel, August 16, 2011.

14 Jenkins.

15 Personal interview with Brian McKinney, June 24, 2011.

16 Ibid.

17 Personal interview with Ken Green, July 26, 2011.

18 Personal interview with Clare Neri, July 26, 2011.

19 Personal interview with Gina Davidson, June 24, 2011.

20 The employee was so shaken by the incident that the individual did not wish to be interviewed.

21 Personal interview with Roberta, June 24, 2011. The witness requested that her last name be withheld.

22 Personal interview Diane Watson, July 26, 2011.

23 Personal interview with Andrew Naylor, June 24, 2011.

Chapter Two: Haunted Hostelries

1 Another version has it that the warning came from a dark, shadowy figure.

2 Personal interview with Burt Heacock, July 3, 2011.

3 Personal interview with Barrie Fletcher, July 3, 2011.

4 The shape might not have been turning, but dematerializing, thus seeming to decrease its profile.

5 Heacock.

6 Fletcher.

7 Heacock.

8 Quoted in Heacock. The smell, though, was very different from the scent sprayed upstairs—this was a heavy masculine odour that was vaguely similar to a men's cologne.

9 Quoted in Heacock.

10 Quoted in Fletcher.

11 Ibid.

12 Ibid.

13 Heacock.

14 Quoted in Heacock.

15 Fletcher.

16 Fletcher.

17 Quoted in Heacock.

18 Personal interview with Thomas, July 3, 2011. Last name withheld.

19 For the fascinating story of Henry Hoet and the building of his house, see James Musson, *Grand Delusions: Henry Hoet and Cobblestone Manor*. The book is available through www.brightest-pebble.com.

20 Personal interview with Marsha Negrych, July 5, 2011.

21 Personal interview with Ivan Negrych, July 5, 2011.

22 Personal interview with Les Shoemaker, July 19, 2011. Les's skepticism is not surprising, for many people are not affected by preternatural events and find it difficult to accept the accounts of others who have encountered the paranormal. Les's wife, Mely, is more sensitive and apparently has a better recollection of the ghostly occurrences that have taken place there, but she was away at the time of my visit to the bed and breakfast.

23 Ibid.

24 Personal interviews with Tanica and Ashley Drinkle, July 21, 2011.

25 Personal interview with Jean Aquin, July 15, 2011.

26 The final report of the investigation into the fire was not made public.

27 It is lore handed down during a relatively short time, and within the circumscribed community of the hotel. The story appears to be a straightforward account without obvious embellishment. Further, an employee who was on leave at the time of the incident recalls hearing the story from her co-workers.

28 Telephone interview with Janet Wagner, May 15, 2012.

29 Personal interview with Shandel Brandics, July 21, 2011.

30 Wagner.

31 Personal interview with Fenny Harpell, July 22, 2011.

32 Brandics.

33 Personal interview with Rick Bart, July 29, 2011.

34 McLelland is now general manager of the Taber Heritage Inn.

Chapter Three: Haunted Houses

1 Telephone interview with Ken Bruce, January 26, 1911.

2 Email, January 31, 2011. Name withheld at correspondent's request.

3 For gravity to have been the cause, the door would have had to swing inward at a steep angle.

4 Cited in Ken Bruce, telephone interview, November 20, 2006.

5 Victoria *Daily Colonist*, February 28,1932.

6 Personal interview with Bruce Pinard, February 26, 2011.

7 Over sixty years after he sold the property, local legend credited Bell as the original owner of the house.

8 Personal interview with Drew Fidoe, January 4, 2011.

9 Personal interview with Marie Fidoe, January 4, 2011.

10 Personal interview with Lynda Gold, January 25, 2011.

11 Telephone interview with Jane Dawe, December 6, 2010.

12 Pat Dufour and Nancy Brown, "Two Children Slain, Mother Kills Self," *Times Colonist*, (Victoria, BC), October 22, 1984.

Chapter Four: Haunted Museums

1 Personal interview with Tim White, April 6, 2011.

2 Ibid.

3 Mission *Fraser Valley Record*, March 12, 1980. The newspaper has printed the wrong spelling of the diver's name. See British Columbia Archives, Vital Events Indexes, Death Registration Index, microfilm no. B13602 (GSU # 2051386).

4 Personal interview with Jim Hinds, May 20, 2011.

5   It has not been possible to discover that many deaths have taken place within the powerhouse itself, which adds credence to the belief that many of these ghosts have no direct connection with the facility. One cannot, however, discount the fact that, given the highly charged environment, this haunting involves motile entities that might have died in the old power station but are not limited to the building itself.

6   Quoted in a personal interview with Tim White, March 7, 2012.

7   Personal interview with Tim White, April 6, 2011.

8   Personal interview with Janis Schultz, April 24, 2011.

9   White, 2011.

10 *Vancouver Sun*, April 14, 1965.

11 Personal interview with Janis Schultz, March 7, 2012.

12 Jeff Small, quoted in Richard Amery, "A Sunday Night Fright," *Lethbridge Sun Times*, October 27, 2010, accessed January 3, 2014, http://www.lethsuntimes.com/Cover-Story/a-sunday-night-fright.html.

13 Personal interview with Belinda Crowson, July 5, 2011.

14 Quoted in Crowson.

15 It is certainly questionable whether the spirit that haunts the site is a nurse, for she has never been seen. However, it is often the case where paranormal activity occurs in a hospital or former hospital that the ghosts of nurses are associated with the haunting.

16 The concrete basement was not added until 1931.

17 Coincidentally, another person named Charles Gathercole was a settler in the south side of the city, a farmer about seven years younger than the dry goods clerk. Whether the two men with unusual last names were related or not has never been discovered.

18 Quoted in an interview with Dianne Wilson, July 10, 2011.

19 Interview with Dianne Wilson, July 10, 2011.

Chapter Five: Spirits in a Glass

1   Personal interview with Dennis Madden, June 23, 2006.

2   Ibid.

3   The human psyche demands order. Horror movies frequently use arrhythmic raps upon doors to build tension within their audiences. Whoever or whatever was producing the sounds that night appeared to be attempting to frighten the two men present.

4   Madden, 2006.

5   Personal interview with Jason Gieck, June 23, 2006.

6   Personal interview with Michelle Martin, June 23, 2006.

7   According to one psychic, the ghost is that of a small girl, not a little boy.

8   Personal interview with Samantha McLellan, June 28, 2011.

9   Madden, 2006.

10 McLellan.

11 Personal interview with Dennis Madden, June 28, 2011.

12 Union Cemetery Index, James "Cappy" Smart, accessed January 3, 2014, http://people.ucalgary.ca/~dsucha/cappy.html.

13 Years after the incident, although each man clearly recalls the event, the two witnesses do not agree on the contents of the pail. Doug believes it contained barbecue sauce.

14 Personal interview with Chuck Rose, July 29, 2011.

15 Quoted in Rose.

16 Chuck did not at first rule out the possibility that the night cleaning staff were playing practical jokes. However, they have denied tampering with the stove.

17 Personal interview with Sheena McAllister, June 29, 2011.

18 Personal interview with Matt Gagat, June 29, 2011.

19 Some staff members do not believe this spectre is a residual haunting, but that it takes pleasure in scaring unsuspecting male patrons.

20 McAllister.

21 Personal interview with Heather Herfft, June 29, 2011.

22 McAllister.

23 Herfft.

24 McAllister.

25 Personal interview with Barbara Mercer, July 20, 2011.

26 Personal interview with Scarlett Mercer, July 20, 2011.

Chapter Six: Haunted Hospitals

1   Research continued at Crease Clinic until the middle 1960s, when volunteer staff members were given hallucinogenic drugs as part of a double-blind study. The effects of the drugs proved injurious to some of the participants.

2   Corinna Carlson, "Do You Believe in Ghosts?" accessed January 3, 2014, http://gusgreeper.com/?s=Do+You+Believe+in+Ghosts%3F.

3   "Shelf Life Wraps Successfully—Despite the Riverview ghosts," accessed January 3, 2014, http://www.scifislacker.com/news/movie_shelf_life.shtml. (*Subhuman* was also released as *Shelf Life*.)

4   While the sighting or sightings may be based on at least one actual event, the information given by the child is supplied apparently through a Ouija board, a singularly unreliable source of information.

5   Personal interview with Glenda Coombs, July 6, 2011.

6   Ibid.

7   Personal interview with Adele Christen, July 6, 2011.

8   Personal interview with Moe Andruschak, July 6, 2011.

9   Personal interview with Janna Grant, July 6, 2011.

[10] The Columbia Tower was built on the site of a much older facility.
[11] Personal interview with Sonia Lee, April 10, 2011.

Chapter Seven: More Haunted Houses
[1] Rail service was via the Shuswap and Okanagan Railway, and the CPR mainline.
[2] *Vernon News*, April 5, 1894.
[3] Personal interview with Gabriel Newman, June 27, 2011. For information on the tour, see www.ghosttoursofvernon.com.
[4] Quoted in Newman.
[5] Paranormal activity is often activated or enhanced by changes to the interior structure of a building.
[6] Telephone interview with Carol Giesbrecht, January 17, 2007.
[7] Telephone interview with Ken Norris, August 10, 2011.
[8] Personal interview with Candis Kirkpatrick, July 8, 2011.
[9] Personal interview with Brenda McPhedran, July 12, 2011.
[10] Telephone interview with Donna McArthur, January 24, 2011.

Chapter Eight: Cemetery Ghosts
[1] See *Haunted Kamloops* (Kamloops, BC: Kamloops Museum & Archives [2011]).
[2] For the story of the Sagebrush Theatre haunting, see my book *Ghosts: More Eerie Encounters*, 88–93.
[3] Personal interview with Melissa Baker, June 24, 2011.
[4] Quoted in the Regina *Leader-Post*, November 30, 1938.
[5] Ibid.
[6] Regina *Leader-Post*, December 1, 1938.
[7] One of Sir Winston Churchill most famous quotes from an October 1939 speech concerning the future action of Russia.

Chapter Nine: Visitations
[1] Jean Manifold, e-mail message to author, July 5, 2011.

Chapter Ten: Other Haunts
[1] Quoted in telephone interview with Patricia Melsted-Chabot, August 8, 2011.
[2] Patricia Melsted-Chabot, e-mail message to author, June 25, 2011.
[3] Personal interview with Lynda Wood, February 4, 2011.

Unpublished

Beale Papers, Saskatchewan Archives, Regina.

Mohr Papers, Vernon City Archives, Vernon, BC.

Yarbo Papers, Saskatchewan Archives, Regina.

Published

Auerbach, Loyd. *ESP, Hauntings and Poltergeists: A Parapsychologist's Handbook*. New York: Warner Books, 1986.

———. *Hauntings & Poltergeists: A Ghost Hunter's Guide*. Berkeley, CA: Ronin Publishing, 2004.

———. *A Paranormal Casebook: Ghost Hunting in the New Millennium*. Dallas: Atriad Press, 2005.

Belanger, Jeff. *The World's Most Haunted Places: From the Secret Files of Ghostvillage.com*. Franklin Lakes, NJ: New Page Books, 2004.

Belyk, Robert C. *Ghosts: More Eerie Encounters*. Victoria, BC: TouchWood Editions, 2006.

———. *Ghosts: True Tales of Eerie Encounters*. Victoria, BC: TouchWood Editions, 2006. First published 1990 by Horsdal & Schubart.

Broughton, Richard S. *Parapsychology: The Controversial Science*. New York: Ballantine Books, 1991.

Bruce, H. Addington. *Historic Ghosts and Ghost Hunters*. New York: Moffat, Yard & Company, 1908. Kindle edition.

Christensen, Jo-Anne. *Ghost Stories of Saskatchewan*. Toronto: Hounslow, 1995.

———. *Ghost Stories of Saskatchewan 3*. Toronto: Dundurn Press, 2009.

Cohen, Daniel. *Encyclopedia of Ghosts*. London: Michael O'Mara Books, 1989.

Day, Sharon. *Was that a Ghost?* n.p. 2011. Kindle edition.

Evans, Hilary, and Patrick Huyghe. *The Field Guide to Ghosts and Other Apparitions*. New York: Quill, 2000.

Felton, D. *Haunted Greece and Rome: Ghost Stories from Classical Antiquity*. Austin: University of Texas Press, 1999. Google Play Book edition.

Fraser, Simon. "Journal of a Voyage from the Rocky Mountains to the Pacific Ocean Performed in the Year 1808, 26 May 1808." In *The Letters and Journals of Simon Fraser, 1806–1808*, ed. W. Kaye Lamb (Toronto: Dundurn, 2007.)

Haining, Peter. *A Dictionary of Ghosts*. New York: Dorset Press, 1993.

———. *Ghosts: The Illustrated History*. London: Treasure Press, 1987.

Hapgood, Sarah. *The World's Great Ghost and Poltergeist Stories*. Toronto: Foulsham, 1994.

"Haunted Cemeteries in Illinois," Anna Marie Bowman Hub Pages, accessed January 24, 2013, anna-marie-bowman.hubpages.com/hub/Haunted-Cemeteries-In-Illinois.

Innes, Brian. *Ghost Sightings*. London: Brown Books, 1996.

Jackson, Robert. *Great Mysteries: Ghosts*. New York: Smithmark, 1992.

Kamloops Museum & Archives. *Haunted Kamloops*. Kamloops, BC: Kamloops Museum & Archives, 2011.

Kuhn, Thomas S. *The Structure of Scientific Revolutions*. 3rd ed. Chicago: University of Chicago Press, 1996.

Ludlam, Harry, ed. *Elliott O'Donnell's Casebook of Ghosts*. Secaucus, NJ: Castle Books, 1989.

Musson, James. *Grand Delusions: Henry Hoet and Cobblestone Manor*. Edmonton: Brightest Pebble, 1995.

Rae-Ellis, Vivienne, ed. *True Ghost Stories of Our Own Time*. London: Faber and Faber, 1990.

Rainey, Rich. *Haunted History*. New York: Warner Books, 1992.

Roll, William. *The Poltergeist*. New York: Nelson Doubleday, 1972.

Smith, Susy. *Prominent American Ghosts*. New York: The World Publishing Company, 1967.

Stanley, Meg, and Hugh Wilson. *Station Normal: The Power of the Stave River*. Vancouver: Douglas & McIntyre, 2001.

Thay, Edrick. *Haunted Cemeteries: True Tales from beyond the Grave*. Edmonton: Ghost House Books, 2004.

Williams, Bryan, and Annalisa Ventola. *Poltergeist Phenomena: A Primer on Parapsychological Research and Perspectives*. publicparapsychology.org/Public Parapsych/Poltergeist Phenomena Primer Final.pdf.

Williams, Bryan, Annalisa Ventola, and Mike Wilson. *Apparitional Experiences: A Primer on Parapsychological Research and Perspectives*. publicparapsychology. blogspot.ca/2010/03/download-apparitional-experiences.html.

Winer, Richard, and Nancy Osborn. *Haunted Houses*. New York: Bantam Books, 1979.

Moe Andruschak

Jean Aquin

Linda Aquin

Melissa Baker

Rick Bart

Joyce Bonertz

Shandel Brandics

Ken Bruce

Adele Christen

Maureen Clayton

Glenda Coombs

Belinda Crowson

Terry Daniel

Jane Dawe

Judy Douglas

Ashley Drinkle

Tanica Drinkle

Gina Davidson

Drew Fidoe

Marie Fidoe

Barrie Fletcher

Matt Gagat

Jason Gieck

Carol Giesbrecht

Lynda Gold

Janna Grant

Ken Green

Fenny Harpell

Burt Heacock

Heather Herfft

Jim Hinds

Andy Jenkins

Gordon Juli

Pat Kammerer

Candis Kirkpatrick

Sonia Lee

Dennis Madden

Jean Manifold

Michelle Martin

Sheena McAllister

Donna McArthur

Brian McKinney

Debbie McKinney

Samantha McLellan

Tyrel McLelland

Brenda McPhedran

Melissa Melindi

Patricia Melsted-Chabot

Barbara Mercer

Scarlett Mercer

Andrew Naylor

Ivan Negrych

Marsha Negrych

Clare Neri

Gabriel Newman

Ken Norris

Bruce Pinard

Lisa Regan

Dennis Roberge

Chuck Rose

Janis Schultz

Diana Segboer

Les Shoemaker

Janet Wagner

Diane Watson

Tim White

Dianne Wilson

Lynda Wood

Roberta (last name withheld)

Thomas (last name withheld)

I would like to thank all the people whom I interviewed and who gave me their fascinating accounts. I would particularly like to thank Jim and Gloria McRae for their kindness and hospitality; the staff at the High River Centennial Archives; Valerie Billesberger of the Mission Community Archives; Allison White and Valerie Patenaude of the Maple Ridge Museum and Community Archives; Ron Candy, Barbara Bell, and Liz Allison of the Greater Vernon Museum and Archives; Brent Hutchinson and Neena Yellow Face of the Empress Theatre; and Lothar Malmberg of the Drumheller Guided Ghost Walk Tour. I would like to thank Diane, my wife, who was photographer, travelling companion, itinerary planner, and co-driver during our journey across western Canada. I appreciate all the work she has so tirelessly given toward the completion of this project. Finally, I would like to express my sincere appreciation to my editor, Marlyn Horsdal, for her contribution, not only to this collection of ghost stories but also to the completion of many of my earlier books.

ROBERT C. BELYK is an author who is particularly interested in western history and the paranormal. He has written seven books, including *Ghosts: True Stories from British Columbia, Ghosts II: More True Stories from British Columbia, Great Shipwrecks of the Pacific Coast, Ghosts: True Tales of Eerie Encounters*, and *Ghosts: More Eerie Encounters*. He writes for publications such as *Canadian West, Photo Life, British Columbia History, Beautiful British Columbia, Wild West*, and *True West*. Born in Vancouver, Robert grew up in Burnaby not far from Still Creek and the bog lands then known as "The Flats." It was a wild place where there were few trespassers, and he and his friends had to be careful where they stepped lest they sunk up to their knees in the black ooze or brushed against the stinging nettle growing near the creek. When dark winter clouds hung low over Burnaby Lake, it was an eerie place, for in the wind, you could hear the voices of the First Nations people who once hunted water birds there. Visit Robert at Haunts West, www.hauntswest.com.